5.00
H

(64-15044) 6-15-65

A
SOUTHERN
PROPHECY

The Prosperity of the South
Dependent upon the Elevation of the Negro
(1889)

A

SOUTHERN
PROPHECY

The Prosperity of the South
Depend at upon the Elevation of the Negro
(1889)

LEWIS H. BLAIR

A
SOUTHERN
PROPHECY

The Prosperity of the South
Dependent upon the Elevation of the Negro
(1889)

By
LEWIS H. BLAIR

Edited with an Introduction by
C. VANN WOODWARD

LITTLE, BROWN AND COMPANY · BOSTON · TORONTO

Published simultaneously in Canada
by Little, Brown & Company (Canada) Limited

PRINTED IN THE UNITED STATES OF AMERICA

To

LYNDON BAINES JOHNSON

In Hope of the Fulfillment

of

A Southern Prophecy

Editor's Note

Lewis H. Blair evidently stood in need of an able proofreader, and his book as originally published shows it. To remedy this need the following edition has silently corrected typographical errors, slips in spelling, arithmetic and grammar, and faults in style, punctuation, and capitalization. The intent throughout has been to make his meaning clear and increase readability.

I am especially indebted to Professor Charles E. Wynes of the University of Georgia for information and advice in this work. His excellent book, *Race Relations in Virginia, 1870-1902*, supplied much needed background material. But I am indebted to him for more than that. Upon learning that I was working on this edition, he exceeded the common bounds of scholarly courtesy and made available to me the manuscript of a biographical essay, "Lewis Harvie Blair, Virginia Reformer: The Uplift of the Negro and Southern Prosperity," which will be found in the January 1964 number of the *Virginia Magazine of History and Biography*. I am deeply grateful to him.

C. V. W.

Contents

Contents

INTRODUCTION

LEWIS H. BLAIR, PROPHET WITHOUT HONOR

C. Vann Woodward

It is now three quarters of a century since Lewis Harvie Blair of Richmond, Virginia, published his book in defense of Negro equality. An uncompromising attack on racial segregation, discrimination, and injustice of any kind, his book demanded full civil rights for the Negro, equal access to hotels, theaters, and all places of amusement and public accommodations, unrestricted franchise and political rights, as well as integration of churches and public schools. Accompanying these demands was a blistering and iconoclastic attack on the dogmas of white supremacy and Negro inferiority, the plantation legend of slavery, the paternalistic tradition of race relations, the black-domination picture of Reconstruction, and the complacent optimism of the New South school of economists.

Published in 1889, Blair's *Prosperity of the South Dependent upon the Elevation of the Negro* attracted little attention and had little influence. It was soon forgotten and has been neglected ever since. The quick oblivion is not hard to explain. The book appeared not long before the great racist reaction that overtook the country in the 1890's. In the South the reaction found expression in white supremacy propaganda, segregation laws, poll taxes, literacy and property tests, white primaries and other devices for disfranchising the Negroes. It was accompanied by an increase in lynching, riots, and other forms of violence against the minority race. It resulted in driving the Negro from all forums and avenues of political life, in stripping him of many of the civil rights and defenses he had gained through the Reconstruction amendments, and in reducing him to a despised and segregated outcast.

By the end of the century the South had reached a consensus on race policy. Its mind was closed. The debate was over. Dissent was frowned down or smashed. Conformity was demanded of all. The ensuing rigidity of regional attitude is reminiscent of that which occurred over the slavery issue in the early 1830's. And under these circumstances a book by a Southerner of authentic lineage and high standing that challenged every dogma of the new consensus from top to bottom was about as welcome and popular as a red-hot abolitionist tract by a comparable Southern author in the 1850's.

But in 1889 the great freeze had not yet taken place. Alternatives were still available. Real choices had to be made. Many of those issues about which there was soon to be such stiff conformity and incorrigible rigidity were still open questions. And in Virginia there was rather more hesitancy about closing off the debate and clamping down conformity than there was in other Southern states.

Charles E. Wynes, the most recent and thorough student of race relations in Virginia, finds that "the most distinguishing factor in the complexity of social relations between the races was that of inconsistency. From 1870-1900, there was no generally accepted code of racial mores." During that period of thirty years, according to this scholar, "at no time was it the general demand of the white populace that the Negro be disfranchised and white supremacy made the law of the land." The era of Jim Crow was still to come, and its first formal appearance in Virginia was not until 1900, when a law requiring the separation of the races on railroad cars was adopted. Up until that time, according to Mr. Wynes, "the Negro sat where he pleased and among the white passengers on perhaps a majority of the state's railroads." The same was true of streetcars and, with greater variation and more exceptions, of other public accommodations and places of entertainment. While he often encountered rebuff and even eviction, "occasionally the Negro met no segregation when he entered restaurants, bars, waiting rooms, theatres, and other public places of amusement." Whatever the risks and uncertainties and the crosscurrents of ambivalence and ambiguity, there was still a considerable range of flexibility, tolerance, and uninhibited contact and association in relations between the races in Virginia.[1]

In the political life of the state during this period the Negroes, being a majority of the population in forty of the ninety-nine counties, played a prominent and sometimes crucial part. They held numer-

[1] Charles Wynes, *Race Relations in Virginia, 1870-1902* (Charlottesville, 1961), especially pp. 68, 149-150.

ous public offices, elective and appointive. There were Negro members of the General Assembly, the oldest representative legislative body in the New World, in every session from 1869 to 1891. [2] Negroes voted in large numbers, and while they were overwhelmingly Republican, their votes were sought by both of the major parties and with striking success by two important third parties in the period, the Readjusters and the Populists. A split between radicals and moderates in the Republican party deprived the Negroes of the prominent role they played during Reconstruction in some other Southern states. But they compensated for this in large measure by the part they played in the Readjuster party, which drove the conservatives from power in 1879 and took control of the state until 1883. Combining with impoverished and discontented white farmers and workers in support of the Readjusters, the Negroes assisted in giving Virginia a foretaste of Populism and the most liberal reform administration the state ever had — before or since. Among the relics of the old regime swept away by the reformers were the whipping post, the poll tax as a voting requirement, and official connivance at dueling. In addition, the Readjusters rejuvenated the impoverished public schools, founded a Negro college, chartered labor unions, reformed the laws to tax privileged corporations, and in general reversed Virginia's retreat to ante-bellum reactionism and advanced the state to a leading position among Southern states.

Returning to power in 1884, the conservatives

[2] Luther P. Jackson, *Negro Office-Holders in Virginia, 1865-1895* (Norfolk, 1945).

rushed through a new election law designed to de-
fraud Negro voters and invite ballot-box corruption.
The law was effectively used for this purpose, but
Negro political strength still remained formidable. In
the presidential election of 1888 the Democratic can-
didate won by a narrow margin, with 151,979 for
Cleveland, and 150,449 for Harrison. In the same
year the first (and last) Negro, John Mercer Langs-
ton, was elected to Congress from Virginia. At the
same time the people of the state voted down a proposal to hold a convention to amend the liberal Reconstruction Constitution of 1868, a move that would
have made possible the curtailment of Negro suffrage.

Such was the temper of mind, the balance of forces,
and the accommodation of races in Virginia in 1889.
It was one of the pivotal moments of history when
public commitment and decision were still in suspense,
when to all appearances the balance could swing
either way. Voices of reaction, racism, and fanaticism
were already calling for extreme measures — for disfranchisement, for segregation, for rigid conformity
of white supremacy and a closed society. Their influence was already being felt in the lower South and
they were at work in the upper South as well. But in
most of the Southern states, and in Virginia particularly, there was still strong resistance to the fanatics.
There were even Southerners who denounced the
existing compromise of racial accommodation and
called for radical advance to a new order of equal
rights and racial justice. They were few in number, but there was a willingness to hear them out.
The situation was, for the moment, still fluid. There

was a disposition to suspend judgment, to consider alternatives, and to ponder the future with an open mind.

Assuming the normal risks of historical comparisons, one might profitably think in this connection of another pivotal moment in racial relations that occurred in Virginia nearly two generations earlier, in 1832. The slave insurrection of August, 1831, in Southampton County led by Nat Turner had horrified and shaken Virginia profoundly, and the shock permeated the whole South. Disturbed and sobered, Virginians opened a searching, unrestrained, and thorough public debate on the nature and evils of slavery and the needs and means of abolishing the institution. When the legislature met in Richmond in December a committee was appointed to consider the question, and in January a formal debate explored every aspect of slavery — its incompatibility with natural rights and human dignity, its responsibility for economic backwardness, its damage to white manners and morals as well as to Negro welfare and personality. "The institution was denounced as never before," according to one historian; "it was condemned wholesale fashion by legal representatives of a slave-holding people." Among the opponents of slavery were the governor of the state, the editors of the two leading papers of Richmond, a son of John Marshall, and a grandson of Thomas Jefferson. It has been called the "final and most brilliant of the Southern attempts to abolish slavery," but it failed. A majority of the legislature favored some form of abolition, but was unable to agree on the time or the method. The moment passed. Virginia took the path that led to a closed society, a rigid conformity, and a last-ditch defense of the peculiar institution.[3]

Two generations later, in the new debates over the future of race relations, Lewis Blair occupied an extreme position toward the left. But he was not without Southern support for many of his views. Writing in 1886, Noah K. Davis, a philosophy professor at the University of Virginia, said: "What shall we care whether the laws, so they be laws, be made by white or black. We want in Congress men of capacity, honesty, strength. Color is non-essential. . . . The time may come when a Negro shall be our Secretary of State; and who will be foolish enough to object?" He drew the line at social intercourse, but predicted that, "We shall see, or our children shall see, white servants and laborers under Negro employers. Resistance would be vain, and regret senseless. Brains, not color, must settle rank." [4]

Of greater importance as a Southern champion of Negro rights was the Louisiana novelist George W. Cable. Writing and lecturing with great conviction and passion through the 1880's and early 1890's, Cable spoke out against every form of injustice toward the Negro — whether by police or church, in schools or in prisons, at the polls or on the job, by mobs or by courts. If he spared Southern sensibilities on the issue of social intercourse, it was out of strategy.[5]

3 Joseph C. Roberts, *The Road from Monticello: A Study of the Virginia Slavery Debate of 1832* (Durham, 1941), pp. 11-18.

4 Noah K. Davis, "The Negro in the South," *Forum* I (April, 1886), pp. 133-135.

5 George W. Cable, *The Silent South* (New York, 1885) and *The Negro Question* (New York, 1890).

A more negative and phlegmatic restraint upon the advance of racist fanaticism came from some of Blair's own social class. They shared none of his equalitarian convictions, but from the security of their own social position they could not regard the Negro as a threat to the social order and could not understand the racial phobias and hysterias that afflicted lower classes of whites. They sometimes found the Negro vote adaptable to their political maneuvers. Out of their paternalistic tradition they deplored violence against Negroes and occasionally provided effective protection against movements to disfranchise, humiliate, or segregate them. Even conservative papers such as the Charleston *News and Courier* could, as late as 1898, print indignant editorials on the stupidity of the demand for Jim Crow laws.

Unexpected support for Negro rights from a lower order of white society was recruited by the Populist movement in the early 1890's. The Populist approach to the Negro was neither paternalistic nor humanitarian but pragmatic and economic. Caught in the pinch of agrarian depression, white and black farmers formed a political brotherhood on the kinship of common grievances and common oppressors. In their efforts to win and hold their Negro supporters, the Populists fought for Negro civil and political rights and offered the Negroes a warmer political fellowship and greater political equality than they had ever received before.

In none of these camps — the patricians, the Populists, the liberals, or the humanitarians — could there be found a champion of Negro rights who went quite so far in the 1880's and 1890's as the curious

Richmond merchant aristocrat, Lewis Blair. Indeed, it would be difficult if not impossible in that period to find his match in any part of the country.

Lewis Harvie Blair was born in Richmond on June 21, 1834, and died there on November 26, 1916. By the time his generation came along, the branches of the Blair family tree were laden with distinguished names and public honors. The Blair name began to figure prominently in colonial times and continued to grow in distinction through the Civil War years. It was borne by prominent theologians, college presidents, generals, editors, and politicians of national and local importance, including congressmen, senators, cabinet members, and presidential aspirants.

The branch of the family from which Lewis was descended was started in America by John Blair, his great-grandfather, who was born in Ireland in 1720 and emigrated as a child with his older brother Samuel.[6] Both brothers received a classical education at an academy near Philadelphia, both became licensed and ordained Presbyterian ministers at an early age, and both fell under the influence of the evangelist George Whitefield and the Great Awakening. John Blair held the first chair of theology at Princeton, then called the College of New Jersey, from which he had received an honorary degree in 1760. He also served Princeton as a trustee, as vice-president, and for two years as acting president.

[6] For this and much genealogical information that follows, I rely mainly on Louisa Coleman Gordon Blair (ed.), *Blairs of Richmond, Virginia: The Descendants of Reverend John Durburrow Blair and Mary Winston Blair, His Wife* (Richmond, 1933).

Two of John's sons moved to Virginia before the end of the Revolution. James left the state early to settle in Kentucky and found the powerful political family that included his son Francis Preston Blair, Francis Preston, Jr., and Montgomery. John Durburrow Blair, the other son, after graduating in 1775 from Princeton, where he served as tutor, and seeing service with the Revolutionary army, came to Hanover County, Virginia, in 1780 at the age of twenty-one as president of Washington Henry Academy. About ten years later he moved to Richmond to open a classical school and serve the city as its only Presbyterian minister. Having no church in which to preach, he resorted to the Hall of the House of Delegates in Mr. Jefferson's newly completed State Capitol and for years met his congregation in that elegantly classical temple. By this time the fires of the Great Awakening had burned low and appeared to have left few sparks in the bosom of the Reverend Mr. Blair. His disposition was described as "amiable, his temper sweet," and he is reported to have written "many merry notes in verse to his friends that did not lack wit." An affectionate memoir quotes scores of his letters written in rhyming jingles, some in Latin, that give an engaging picture of the hunting, fishing parson. His ministry did not go uncriticized. His critics called him "a wine bibber, a friend of publicans and sinners," and declared that "the fruits of his ministry were not apparent." [7]

The minister's son, John Geddes Blair, born in 1787, was the cashier of a Richmond bank and appears to

[7] *Ibid.*, pp. 87-96; see also George Wythe Munford, *The Two Parsons* (Richmond, 1884), *passim*.

have contented himself with simple pleasures and a rather active domestic life. He was the father of thirteen children, of whom Lewis Harvie was the eleventh. Lewis described his father as a "courteous gentleman," a man of "refined taste and good intelligence" with minor gifts in the arts. "He played sweetly on the flute," remembered Lewis, "sang fairly well, and wrote quite pleasing lines. He was sociable, belonged to an instrumental musical society which met at his house, to a quoit club, composed of prominent gentlemen, and to the Richmond Blues, with whom he took the field in the War of 1812." One enigmatic sidelight on the character of his father is furnished in a description Lewis wrote of his mother, Sarah Anne Eyre Heron Blair. He describes her as being "pretty as a maiden, matron, and old lady," and then adds: "She was a firmer texture than father." [8]

John, the flute player of infirm texture, departed this life on March 7, 1851, leaving a widow and ten surviving children to be supported by an estate that was somewhat less than adequate to the demands upon it. As a result Lewis, not quite seventeen at the time of his father's death, dropped out of school and went to work, never to continue his education. During the ten years preceding the Civil War he turned his hand to a number of jobs under private and government employment. His first was that of clerk to his brother, a captain in the army, then stationed on the Texas frontier, where Lewis served from 1851 to 1855. He then returned to Richmond to work for a merchant a couple of years and in 1857 took a gov-

[8] "Autobiography of Lewis H. Blair," quoted in Blair (ed.), *Blairs of Richmond*, p. 10n.

ernment job as assistant to a lighthouse engineer on the Great Lakes.[9]

Lewis quit the lonely lighthouse work early in 1860 and went back to Richmond seeking to establish himself in business. Before he had got a start, however, the war came and disarranged his life again. He enlisted as a private in the Confederate army in March, 1862, just ahead of the draft. He served undramatically with artillery and cavalry units for two years and for the remainder of the war as adjutant to the commander of a cavalry division. What the experience meant to him at the time is unclear, but his later description of his military service is revealing: "more than three years wasted in the vain effort to maintain that most monstrous institution, African slavery, the real, tho' States Rights were the ostensible cause of the War." [10]

After Appomattox he returned to find the city of his fathers in ashes and his state and region in ruins. He was nearly thirty-one that blighted spring of 1865, with a start in life still to make and a prospect around him bleak enough to discourage even the stout of heart. But Lewis Blair had the sanguine disposition of the tribe of enterprise and business, and instead of despair he felt only a sense of release and optimism. In the opening passage of his book on the Negro he described his hopes on returning to the ruins of Rich-

[9] Blair's recollection of the Texas adventure is preserved by Charles E. Wynes (ed.), "Lewis Harvie Blair: Texas Travels, 1851-1855," *Southwestern Historical Quarterly* LXVI (1962), pp. 262-270.

[10] A full account of Blair's war career, including his quoted comment upon it, is in Charles E. Wynes, "Lewis Harvie Blair, Virginia Reformer," which will be published in January 1964 in the *Virginia Magazine of Biography and History.*

mond. "I fondly imagined a great era of prosperity for the South," he wrote. "Guided by history and by a knowledge of our people and our climatic and physical advantages, I saw in anticipation all her tribulations ended, all her scars healed, and all the ravages of war forgotten, and I beheld the South greater, richer and mightier than when she molded the political policy of the whole country."

Blair admitted twenty-four years after the war that his hopes had been cruelly disappointed. He wrote then that, "instead of beholding the glorious South of my imagination, I see her sons poorer than when war ceased his ravages, weaker than when rehabilitated with her original rights, and with the bitter memories of the past smoldering, if not rankling, in the bosoms of many." He had his own explanation for the disappointment of his hopes and the failure of the South, but that is a later story. The point is that it was during the bitter, iron years of that quarter of a century, for the most part years of depression, poverty, and economic stagnation in the South, that Blair struggled to get his start, founded his fortune, and regained the position his family had once maintained in Richmond. The means he used were several, but the first was a retail, and then a wholesale, grocery business. Then came the manufacture and sale of shoes with headquarters in Richmond and outlets in various towns, and later a thriving business in real estate.

Judging from the style in which he subsequently lived, Blair's struggles did not go unrewarded. His handsome house at 511 East Grace Street was an old one built by Corbin Warwick, who imported its elaborate white Italian marble mantels. Blair added a fashionable mansard-style top story and "a rather modern front porch with a tiled floor." In the eighties and nineties Grace Street was lined with the homes of "old families" and Richmond's great and near-great. Next door to the "Warwick-Blair" house, as it was called, was the home of George E. Barksdale, and nearby lived Randolphs, Branches, Cabells, Pages, Lees, Carys, and "from time to time scores of prominent families." [11] Abner Harvey, a partner in one of Blair's several business enterprises, occupied "one of the largest and handsomest houses," and several of Blair's numerous brothers and sisters were suitably established in the city. Blair married twice. His first wife, Alice Wayles Harrison, bore him seven children; his second, Mattie Ruffin Feild, produced four.

It is clear that the Blairs carried their heads pretty high in Richmond. Lewis more than recouped the family fortunes and status, for it is doubtful that any of the three preceding generations of American Blairs lived in finer style or occupied higher social positions in the city. Whatever may explain the rebellion of this Richmond aristocrat, it was hardly loss of status. Far from being an alienated outcast or a frustrated climber, Lewis Blair was a man of wealth and power and position. More than that, he was at one and the same time "self-made" and "old family" in a society and time when both distinctions counted — especially the latter. And Blair's personality and appearance emphasized identification with the latter. A kinsman who did not share his radical views nevertheless de-

[11] Robert Beverly Munford, Jr., *Richmond Homes and Memories* (Richmond, 1936), pp. 194-201. Sometime later Blair moved to a house on Monument Avenue.

scribed him as "a man of distinguished appearance and of a courtesy in manner that seemed to belong to an even older time." [12]

For all his lack of formal education, Blair was not without cultivated tastes in arts and letters. The same kinsman who conceded his courtly manners wrote: "He was also a gentleman of cultivated intellect who appreciated works of art, and in his Grace Street home were a good many paintings of merit." There were evidently books of merit in the establishment on Grace Street as well, for its master was a reader of some scope and evidently liked to think of himself as abreast of the times. There is little in what he wrote to suggest that he cultivated the taste of his forebears for the classics. He was more interested in modern literature on philosophy, politics, and economics — what the old school called "moral philosophy." He founded his beliefs, he said, on the "school of Adam Smith, Herbert Spencer, and [Ernst] Haeckel." He was something of a skeptic and was reported to entertain "very decided opinions in religious matters, opinions which differ decidedly from those of the majority of his friends and neighbors." [13]

In political matters, with the important exception of questions of civil rights and racial policy, Blair seems to have been more in accord with his neighbors. Enough so at least to have been elected treasurer of the Democratic Committee of Richmond, though his stand for desegregation of the public schools brought a public demand for his resignation from that office in

[12] *Ibid.*, p. 198.
[13] Lyon G. Tyler (ed.), *Encyclopedia of Virginia Biography* (New York, 1915), vol. III, p. 185.

1887.[14] The year before, however, G. P. Putnam's Sons published his first book, *Unwise Laws*,[15] a free trade tract that advanced views familiar enough to the antiprotectionist wing of the Democratic party in the South. He took the extreme laissez-faire position against protective tariff of any kind whatever and held that "all taxes levied shall be exclusively for the benefit of the government and none for the benefit of industries whether infant or ancient." Acknowledging that such a reform would require drastic adjustments in the economy and drive some favored industries out of business, he justified his views with arguments drawn from classical economists of the day.

As a polemicist Blair liked to assume the tone of a hard-boiled realist, a materialist who relied little on the nobler impulses of his fellow man and addressed himself to motives of self-interest. In his opinion "all experience proves that human nature must be interested on its material side before its intellectual and moral interests can be permanently stimulated."[16] The title of his book on the Negro as well as the arguments he stressed illustrate his theory. "You will observe," he pointed out, "that I have appealed little, if at all, to right, justice, morals, or religion, but that the burden of the argument has been dollars and cents." Moreover, "this key-note of appeal to the pocket . . . was deliberately struck." He called for drastic moral reform not "because this was great or

[14] Wynes, *Race Relations in Virginia*, p. 126.
[15] Lewis H. Blair, Unwise *Laws: A Consideration of the Operations of a Protective Tariff upon Industry, Commerce, and Society* (New York, 1886).
[16] Tyler (ed.), *Encyclopedia of Virginia Biography*, vol. III, p. 185.

noble, but simply because it would be profitable." [17] There was nevertheless a good deal of the iron glove on the velvet hand in all this. For behind the rather ostentatious "hard doctrine" he preached, it is not difficult to detect a fierce moral indignation over injustice and strong impulses of ethical idealism.

The Richmond reformer had every reason to be aware of the unpopularity of his racial doctrines in the South. As one of his Virginia contemporaries mildly remarked, "Mr. Blair utters views that in all probability will never achieve popularity south of the Potomac." Blair knew he would be accused of outrageous motives but said he would "patiently bear the odium attached to such charges." "It may seem both invidious and presumptuous to attempt this role," he wrote, "but while frankly admitting that I may be presumptuous, my Southern ancestry, birth, rearing, residence and interest preserve me from the charge of invidiousness." At least no one could call him an outsider.

The role of the iconoclast was obviously congenial to the Blair temperament. This was evident from the zest with which in his book on the Negro problem[18] he pitched into his attack on cherished and hallowed Southern myths, prejudices, credos, anything that stood in the way of the new social doctrine he preached.

His first target was the brightest and most con-

[17] These and all subsequent quotations, unless otherwise noted, are from the edition of *The Prosperity of the South Dependent upon the Elevation of the Negro* which follows.

[18] The book was foreshadowed by a series of articles Blair wrote for the New York *Independent* in the summer of 1887.

spicuous on the contemporary scene — the New South gospel. In 1889 this doctrine had reached a peak of popularity on the eve of the death of its major prophet, Henry W. Grady of Atlanta, the famous orator and editor. Grady left scores of ardent apostles and a host of converts. A message of such cheerful optimism held great attraction for a hope-starved people. Its adherents proclaimed that the cloud of depression and poverty was lifting, that prosperity was rolling in, that great cities like those of the golden East were springing up out of ashes, and manufacturing industries were growing at a magic pace. The great leap forward into the age of industrialization could be accomplished without any painfully protracted period of capital accumulation merely by will power and enough publicity to attract eager Northern and foreign investment capital to abundant natural resources and the cheap labor supply. The era of a depressed, underdeveloped, colonial, raw-material economy was at an end. The states of the late Confederacy, moreover, could march triumphantly into the promised land of industrialization without abandoning many of the values and loyalties and habits of the past. These included white supremacy, the comfortable assurance that the degraded mass of Negroes knew their place and would keep to it, the inexhaustible patience of the impoverished whites, and a large assortment of sentimental ties to the Lost Cause and the old regime.

Blair struck contemptuously at the "brag, and strut, and bluster" of the boosters and the prosperity propaganda of such journals as the Baltimore *Manufacturers' Record*. "Judging by these sheets," he wrote, "one would naturally imagine that the South is a region where poverty is unknown and where everybody is industriously and successfully laying up wealth," that "the South is indeed a happy Arcadia." It was true that New South propaganda had managed to persuade a few Northern journalists and capitalists that it was indeed a "happy Arcadia." But "these gentlemen, having been hurried through hundreds of miles in luxurious palace coaches, have practically been blindfolded as to the condition of the country passed through, and not having their eyes unbandaged until in the midst of furnaces, rolling mills, and all the activities of a manufacturing center, they are dazzled by what they see." The trouble was they had lost sight of "the real South — that is to say, of ninety-five per cent thereof."

Unlike the New South, Lewis Blair's "real South" was a backward land, a land of wretched poverty for "the six millions of Negroes who are in the depths of indigence," as well as the ninety per cent of the whites who had "nothing beyond the commonest necessaries of life," if that. His beloved South was a retarded region of "dilapidated homesteads," of "fenceless plantations," of illiteracy, of chronic underemployment. To prove his contentions and counter those of "devout believers in a new South," he presented comparative statistics on property values, savings, urban growth, manufacturing, and production. Crude as they were as statistics, his figures served to make his point that the South lagged far behind the American procession, that its people were too poor to accumulate savings and industrialize their economy, and that they lived in a quasi-colonial economy of one-

crop agriculture producing raw materials and import-
ing manufactures.

As an active businessman and manufacturer, Blair
knew that there were "many causes conspiring to the
poverty" of the South, and he listed several, conclud-
ing with the degraded status of the Negro. "Each of
these causes," he wrote, "'would greatly retard the
prosperity of the South, or indeed of any country, but
all of them combined, destructive as they would necessarily be to prosperity, are not as serious and as fatal as the last cause, namely: the degradation of the
Negro." It was the most "far-reaching cause of all,"
for it served "to intensify all the other drawbacks."
The slight regard for sanctity of Negro life and civil
rights undermined the sanctity of life and civil rights
for all. And similarly the miserable standards of housing, health, diet, education, and morals imposed on
the degraded race dragged down the standards of the
whole population, whites included, in all these vital
areas. The only way out for the South, therefore, was
the elevation of the Negro — the immediate elevation
of the race.

True to his "hard doctrine" of realism, Blair denied
that he rested his argument on the demands of justice, morality, or religion — however strong those
demands might be. His was the argument of self-
interest based "simply on economic ground, on the
ground of advantage to the whites." The Southern
white man must be convinced that the only way out of
economic stagnation and poverty lay in the elevation
of the Negro — the radical and drastic elevation of
the whole race. This could not be left to slow evolu-
tion. "Man's life is now too short to wait for the natu-

ral process of time." The white man "must hasten nature and take a hand himself." The remedies were of a heroic order, for the Negro "must economically, morally, and socially be born again, and self-respect, hope and intelligence are the trinity that will work out his elevation, and they are also the rule of three to work out our own material regeneration."

But if the Negro were to remain "a despised and degraded creature, speaking with bated breath and bowing with head uncovered," if he were "to remain forever a 'nigger,' an object of undisguised contempt, even to the lowest whites," how could he be expected to develop the self-respect, the hope, the ambition that were essential to striving and effort, self-denial and self-discipline? Why should he be expected to become anything but a clown, a drunkard, and a thief? The South was "a veritable land of caste," and so long as the caste system prevailed the Negro was doomed to servility and humiliation.

Back of the caste system was the myth of white supremacy, and for the pretensions of this dogma Blair had nothing but scorn and contempt. From his reading of history he concluded that "our remote ancestors were as scurvy a lot as ever scourged the earth." Even as late as the Middle Ages they were "a roving set of pirates and freebooters, whose lives were spent in ravishing and then murdering women, in slaying infants and old men, and in reducing to slavery all able-bodied men who escaped the edge of the sword." Those who chanted the praises of white supremacy might do well to remember that they were "the descendants of these monsters."

The Virginia cynic had not entirely freed himself

from the racial credo of his times, for he thought of Negroes as "children" and attributed what progress they had made in America to contact with whites. But on the other hand he rejected the idea of innate or biological inferiority of the race. He was an environmentalist and explained the African's cultural backwardness by reference to "natural surroundings" and "artificial surroundings," by which he meant geographical and cultural environment. Even in Africa environment had produced a wide variety of cultures, some strong and warlike. He wondered "if the surroundings had been reversed whether we would not now be found at the bottom and the blacks at the top of civilization."

Admittedly race prejudice was deeply entrenched among white Americans, but it was "always a weakness," in extreme form "a badge of dishonor," and it must be eradicated. It was nonsense to hold that it was ineradicable, for it had already been abandoned by advanced nations. In England and France and in Latin nations generally the Negro was "under no political or social ban," and in Brazil he was "accorded full social and political equality." In fact, a Virginian who had served as United States consul in Rio in the 1850's assured Blair that "he had danced with Negroes at parties and official receptions" and that many of them "were much more elegantly cultured than he was himself." Yet in our "land of the free" a man with the slightest trace of Negro blood, even one who had "rendered great services to his country or to humanity" and who had been "honored in England, France, and Germany," could never feel safe from "snubs, insults, or even kicks from the superior whites." Such conduct was unworthy of a great nation.

The Virginian was perfectly aware that his people, especially the patricians among them, often prided themselves on acts of kindness and deeds of genuine helpfulness toward individual Negroes and favored families and groups. "But we forget," he wrote, "that our kindness to the Negroes proceeds from the standpoint of condescension, and of assumed caste superiority, and we expect it to be received with humility and from a feeling of acknowledged caste inferiority; and if not so received by the Negroes, they are thought impudent and impertinent, and the foundation of our kindness soon dries up."

The Negro was not deceived by the whites. He knew that "this kindness springs mainly from the same benevolence that prompts consideration for their horses and cattle." He knew it was the reward for quiet and complete submission. He remembered very well that slaves had been treated "pretty much as cattle," that the whites had fought a long and desperate war to keep the Negro enslaved, that they had sought to nullify freedom, that they had opposed Negro enfranchisement, "that civil rights were conferred in spite of all their efforts, and that generally they have opposed everything" tending to the advancement of Negroes.

On the surface the Negro appeared acquiescent and contented and the South peacefully and quietly adjusted in its race relations. But the appearance was deceptive and the adjustment could not continue indefinitely. Shortsighted selfishness and an ancient and modern record of injustice had "raised up an enemy, silent and sullen, at our very doors." The policies of white domination, notwithstanding all paternalistic benevolence and charity and condescension, had produced "in the hearts of six millions of fellow-citizens a vast mass of smoldering enmity and bitterness, only awaiting a favorable opportunity to display itself."

If paternalistic benevolence, condescending kindness, the restraints and indulgences of *noblesse oblige*, and all the charities and back-door integration and half-measures were not the answer, what then was the answer? To Lewis Blair the answer was a complete end to segregation and to all forms of discrimination, favoritism, and exclusion on the ground of race or color. He put it plainly:

The Negro must be allowed free access to all hotels and other places of public entertainment; he must be allowed free admittance to all theatres and other places of public amusement; he must be allowed free entrance to all churches, and in all public and official receptions of president, governor, mayor, etc., he must not be excluded by a hostile caste sentiment. In all these things and in all these places he must, unless we wish to clip his hope and crush his self-respect, be treated precisely like the whites, no better, but no worse.

If this seemed impossible to his fellow Southerners, he called upon them to perform an exercise of the imagination they had never tried before: "Let us put ourselves in the Negro's place," he proposed.

Let us feel when passing good hotels there is no admission here; we dare not go in lest we be kicked out; when entering a theatre to be told to go up in the top gallery, no seat for you in the parquette; when entering an imposing church to be told rudely no place in God's house for you, unless there be a gallery, to which you are sent with indifference; or when seeking to attend an official reception, *your* governor's for instance, to be told brusquely no admittance; and suppose this treatment is continued year after year, and as far as we can see is likely to continue *ad infinitum*, would we not have our pride cut to the quick, and would not our morale be greatly lowered, and would we not be greatly handicapped in all our efforts to get along?

But what of the argument that "theatres, hotels and churches are private property, and that to compel them to receive Negroes on equal terms with whites would be to correct one wrong . . . by committing another." His answer was that although they may be private property, "they are public as regards their creation and their functions, and they are of the nature of railways, which may be private property, but which are public institutions." They were licensed by "the public, which means not some, but all the people, not whites alone, but whites and blacks." They could "as properly refuse accommodation to all whose noses indicate a Semitic origin, all whose names or 'rich brogue' betray Hibernian descent . . . as to refuse similar accommodation to all whose faces are black." To shut the doors of any one of these institutions — whether church or theatre or governor's mansion — "in the faces of any portion of the community is to degrade and to humiliate it."

There was one right, held Blair, that was "the right preservative of all rights." That was the ballot, and it was "as absolutely essential for freedom as is the atmosphere for life." Yet it was denied to a great number of Negro citizens of the lower South, and had been since the overthrow of Reconstruction. This was done sporadically by intimidation and fraud rather than consistently by legal disfranchisement, as it was later to be done. The rationalization of Negro disfranchisement was that it was necessary to prevent Negro domination and assure pure government. In Virginia, North Carolina, and Tennessee at the time Blair was writing, however, the Negroes voted freely and fully. Yet these three states showed "greater progress and prosperity" than the other Southern states, "and certainly as much moral and intellectual development." During the administration of the Readjuster party, Virginia "had so-called Negro rule, but the Commonwealth survived, and, in the opinion of many, was much benefited." Protracted one-party rule in Virginia, as in other Southern states, had produced nepotism, corruption, and numerous treasury defalcations. "The fear of Negro rule in the sense of the alarmists," declared Blair, "is a wild and pernicious chimera," and those "who go around wearing the frightful scare-face" in the name of good government were "doing an untold amount of evil to the South." They not only alienated their fellow citizens, but they put a powerful lever in the hands of sectional foes. "The South would make a tremendous ado . . . if a Northern oligarchy of half the population were to claim and assume the right to vote for the whole population." If the South itself continued to do the same thing, it invited a second Reconstruction. "Better surrender now with the honors of the war, or rather with the honors of right, than to wait for years and then surrender at discretion," he warned.

In tackling the racial problem in the public schools, Blair knew that he faced one of the most sensitive areas of white prejudice and fear. He had remedies to propose, he admitted, "that will clash with all of our preconceived ideas, that will be distasteful and repugnant to our prejudices, but," he stoutly maintained, "not to reason and justice." Therefore, to say that reforms were "distasteful and repugnant is really to say nothing against them," for the whole history of progress and the rise of Christianity itself were "simply an overcoming of the violent prejudices and repugnances of the civilized world." Thus fortified by reason and justice, the intrepid Virginia rationalist set forth his revolutionary proposal:

The remedy proposed is not a bread pill or some soothing syrup, but is a radical and far-reaching one, and is no less than the abandonment of the principle of separate schools, which principle is an efficient and certain mode of dooming to perpetual ignorance both whites and blacks in thinly settled sections.

This was a reform from which even the statesmen of Radical Reconstruction in full possession of power had shied away. And Blair admitted that unless he could convince the whites of the necessity and advantage of the reform, they would "never consent to coeducation [of the races], but will prefer to remain ignorant." He therefore marshaled a wide array of financial, practical, moral, and psychological arguments. Characteristically, he put forward practical reasons of self-interest first, but the real weight of his argument rested upon moral and psychological reasons — some of them quite prophetic and in advance of his time.

The practical and financial arguments were telling. The South was the poorest region of the country with the largest number of children per adult to educate. Its population was not concentrated in towns and cities but widely scattered and dispersed. On top of these enormous burdens was the self-imposed handicap of trying to maintain two separate school systems for the two races, with two corps of teachers and two sets of plants and equipment. The result was a miserably inadequate system, with poor and underpaid teachers, neglected and poorly equipped schools, ill-schooled children, and growing illiteracy. "To fight the battle of education with our present forces and present system of separate schools seems well-nigh hopeless," concluded Blair. To integrate the schools was to relieve the people of part of their burden and improve the schools for both races.

In the second place, separate or segregated schools were morally and psychologically harmful to the children of both races. The damage to the Negro children was most obvious:

Separate schools are a public proclamation to all of African or mixed blood that they are an inferior caste, fundamentally inferior and totally unfit to mingle on terms of equality with the superior caste. That this is not a temporary and ephemeral but a fundamental and caste inferiority is proven by the fact that opposition does not cease when the temporary inferiority ceases, but still operates, however cultured and refined the Negro may be. Hence it follows that separate schools brand the stigma of degradation upon one-half of the population, irrespective of character and culture, and crush their hope and self-respect, without which they can never become useful and valuable citizens.

The feeling of inferiority "thereby taught the blacks cultivates feelings of abasement and of servile fear of all whom they consider superior — sentiments totally destructive of manliness, courage and self-respect."

The damage segregated schools did to white children was less apparent but no less important:

Separate schools poison at its very source the stream whence spring the best and noblest fruits of education . . . At the fountain of education the doctrine of caste, which elsewhere is being successfully combatted, is enshrined in fresh vigor and authority, and it seizes with its rigid, icy grasp the impressible minds of the children, and taints them; and the blind superiority thereby inculcated fosters sentiments of false pride, disregard of the rights of others, and unfeeling haughtiness to all, regardless of color, whom they deem inferiors.

If segregated schooling robbed the Negro children of incentive for achievement, it had the same effect on white children, though from an opposite cause. Since it taught them that "superiority consists in a white skin, they will naturally be satisfied with that kind of superiority, and they will not willingly undergo the tedious, painful and patient ordeal requisite to prepare them for superiority in science, art, literature."

Integrated schools would "emancipate us from this fallacy" and teach both races that "the difference between man and man is not color, but character and conduct." They would dissipate the spirit of "oligarchy, caste, vassalage," and disseminate "correct ideas of personal liberty and equality." They would help remove the brand of degradation from the Negro and the false assumption of superiority from the white and give new incentive for achievement to both.

Those who protested that integration would demoralize the white children "overlook the fact that from earliest childhood they have been subjected to intimate Negro association" with playmates and "the unrestrained influences of Negro nurses at the very time the mind and the heart are most susceptible to influence of every kind." If segregation were the salvation of the whites, it came too late. As for the dangers of demoralization, "History, fiction, the drama, everyday life, all abundantly illustrate the demoralizing effects of the higher upon the lower walks of society. . . . and so it is in the South in the intercourse of the two colors. . . . Demoralization, indeed!"

Looking to the future, Blair saw three alternatives open to the South. The first was to assure Negroes "the whole one hundred per cent" of their rights, so they would be "as free and as equal citizens as the proudest whites." That, he strongly urged, was the way to "peace, happiness, prosperity for all." The second alternative lay in "completely disarming the blacks and reducing them to a condition of complete subordination and degradation." The third lay in half-measures, compromises, and inadequate concessions. Both of the latter alternatives led to "strife, sorrow, adversity for all."

A full retreat to the past, to a cordon sanitaire and an intellectual barricade against criticism and ideas such as the slave regime maintained, was no longer really open to the South. The outside world was now looking over its shoulder and could not be shut out or put off. "We can no more defend our attitude towards the Negroes," he wrote, "than could the Algerian corsairs defend their attitude to the Christian world." The age of caste and privilege was over, for this was "the age of reason." He did not expect to see the walls of caste come tumbling down overnight. "The battle will be long and obstinate," and there would be "many difficulties, delays, and dangers." Nevertheless, he was confident of victory in the end. "We older ones will not see that day," he said, "but our grand-children will, for the light of coming day already irradiates the eastern sky."

As a final word, Blair addressed an admonition and an appeal to the North. Careful as always to appeal to the motive of self-interest, he pointed out that "in a common country one great section cannot languish without the other sections, even the wealthy and prosperous manufacturing sections, suffering also." The North had a vested interest in the welfare of the South, "and *if* the prosperity of the South is dependent upon the elevation of the Negro your prosperity is intimately associated with that of the South," and could not "escape the penalty of the South remaining in a stagnant or declining condition in consequence of the Negroes remaining in a state of degradation." In Blair's opinion, "the greatest impediment in the way of Southerners being willing to elevate the Negro" was the North's own "dereliction of duty towards him." This put into the mouth of Southerners the *argumentum ad hominem*, "the argument that you do so yourself." And so every valid criticism of Southern injustice was nullified by an equally valid charge of Northern hypocrisy.

The Virginian was correct in saying the Negro fared better in the North, but knowing less of that section than his own, he conceded too much in saying that "the Negro can travel anywhere without question, and can, with exceptions, attend churches, theatres, and official receptions, and put up at hotels, without fear of affront." He was on firmer ground in his charges of segregated housing, wretched slums, and exclusion of the Negro from skilled and high-wage jobs. "Caste pursues and cripples the Negro in the North as it does in the South." He called on the North to "clear its skirts of the charge of hypocrisy," for until it did so "the seed it sows may be good, but it will fall upon hard and stony soil."

But what was one to say to Southerners who maintained that such radical changes as he proposed were impossible, that they did too much violence to tradition and to history, that they were too great a change and too sudden a break with the past? Lewis Blair had somehow acquired a feeling for the changing fortunes of history, the inevitability of change, and the ephemerality of institutions. He suggested to Southerners that they had less reason than other Americans to talk so confidently about the imperishability of institutions, the inviolable continuity of history, and the improbability of cataclysmic change. Yankees had more excuse to talk in such fanciful language, for they had been spared the tragic experience of history that the South — and most of the world — had suffered, and they could afford to cherish all sorts of illusions about history that were denied Southerners.

And so the Virginian advised Southerners that they

should be very chary of saying anything is impossible, or that such a thing shall never be, in view of what has taken place and in view of what we have agreed to in the past quarter-century. In that time we have seen slaves made freedmen at the scratch of one man's pen; by a simple "Be it enacted" we have seen freedmen made citizens, legislators, jurors, teachers of youth, etc., etc.; we have seen civil and political society completely changed, and social life profoundly modified; in a word, we are living in a new world, and we have assented to all these fundamental changes that have made the new world.

Why then this sense of dismay and shock over a new era of innovation and change? Such changes as integrated schools for the 1890's would not be "half so shocking" as were the innovations of the 1860's — still fresh in the memory of many — for they included "Negro emancipation, Negro voting, Negro lawmaking, Negroes sitting on juries, Negroes riding in rail and street cars, our lordly selves standing the meanwhile, Negroes sleeping in the same berths on Pullman cars, etc., etc.; but where is our dread of them?" asked Lewis Harvie Blair in 1889. He asked this question rhetorically, at least in part no doubt, but answered it himself: "Dissipated by experience."

That he could have asked such a question and furnished such an answer (and in good faith, I believe) on the eve of the Jim Crow era, when the Negro was so rapidly to disappear from the polls, the legislatures, the juries, the railroad cars, the streetcars, and the

Pullman cars, is not without value to the collector of ironies. It is less a reflection upon his sense of history, however, than upon his gifts for prophecy. We have discovered something worthy of praise in the Virginian's sense of history. And if we can afford to be so generous as to allow him somewhat better than three quarters of a century as a reasonable margin of error, we might yet conceivably award him honors as a minor prophet.

But that is not the end of the story of Lewis Blair as a prophet of race relations. Nor is it the full measure of its irony. Unfortunately, he lived on through the era of reactionary racism and Jim Crowism. More unfortunate still, there exists unimpeachable evidence that the prophet himself was swept up in the storm of reaction he failed to predict and could not foresee. As late as 1898 he was still reaffirming his equalitarian heresies and lamenting the fact that the South seemed more determined than ever to keep the Negro down and that the North was more and more indifferent to his plight. Blair's great change came sometime after that, between 1898 and his death in 1916. Exactly when and exactly why are unknown. But in his private papers (still in private hands) Mr. Wynes has recently found a manuscript of 270 pages, untitled, unsigned and undated, but unmistakably identified by the handwriting as Blair's own. It is a complete and unqualified recantation of his equalitarian and liberal position of 1889 with regard to the Negro. More than that, it is a total reversal of his earlier stand. It will be recalled that in his book he had indicated three alternatives of racial policy open to the South. The first, his own, was "the whole one hundred per cent" of rights and equality; the second, "complete subordination and degradation"; the third, half-measures, compromises and limited concessions. The two latter he had prophesied led to "strife, sorrow, adversity for all." In the undated handwritten manuscript, belatedly rejecting the first, he now chose not the third but the second alternative; he declared that "the only logical position for the Negro is absolute subordination to the whites." Blair's new logic called for repeal of the Fourteenth and Fifteenth Amendments as well as the complete disfranchisement and total segregation of the Negro. He should be treated kindly but always as an inferior creature — permanently and inherently inferior to whites.

The charitable impulse would be to attribute the change to senility, but the fact is that Blair maintained a lively and intelligent sympathy with Wilsonian progressivism up to the end of his days. His new racial views were quite reconcilable with the progressivism of that day, of course, but neither was the result of senility. Another possibility is that his second marriage in 1898, at the age of sixty-four, to a woman half his age who did not share his racial views may have influenced him. But to those who are familiar with this obscure era of Southern history Blair's complete reversal will not seem so strange or unprecedented. Other examples will come to mind. The most prominent were the Southern Populists, who swung from an advanced brand of racial justice (though more limited than Blair's) to an extreme brand of racial injustice — with Tom Watson of Georgia as the classic instance. Blair only proved it could happen in

Virginia too, on the other side of the railroad tracks and in one of the finer mansions. The recantation was never published, but there it is, a sad commentary on the frailty of mind and the infirmity of principle.

It is hard to say now which is the greater biographical enigma, the ringing affirmation of faith in 1889 or the silent recantation of old age. But across the dark years of reaction, years of "strife, sorrow, adversity" that he himself predicted would follow the course he later took, the boldly prophetic pronouncement of '89 stands forth as clear, as relevant, and as challenging as it was when it was published seventy-five years ago.

New Haven, November, 1963

The Prosperity of the South
Dependent upon the Elevation of the Negro
(1889)

The Prosperity of the South
Dependent upon the Elevation of the Negro
(1889)

THE

PROSPERITY OF THE SOUTH

DEPENDENT UPON THE

ELEVATION OF THE NEGRO

———

BY

LEWIS H. BLAIR,

AUTHOR OF

"UNWISE LAWS."

———

RICHMOND, VA.:
EVERETT WADDEY,
1889.

Contents

Preface

In discussing great themes, in contemplating great subjects, it is essential, in order to arrive at a true interpretation or to reach a wise decision, to take into consideration great causes and broad effects.

In the lower realms of animal life we can sever and dissever, and each segment at once begins a new and separate existence entirely independent of its parent form. But when we ascend higher, bisection means destruction, and equally when we approach the grand region of humanity, and its vast concerns, we cannot cut into fragments and discuss each section, as if it had a separate existence, as if it were independent of its connections and surroundings; or if we do, we necessarily remain in the darkness of error, and, instead of walking in pathways illumined by day, we stumble into pitfalls, we flounder in quagmires concealed by the gloom of night.

Now, few themes, few subjects, are or can be of vaster import than the prosperity and happiness, not only of the twelve millions and more souls dwelling in our Southern land, but of the many more and innumerable millions that are to come after us; and, therefore, there is no question that it behooves us to approach with broader views or with a more judicial spirit. This is not a question that can possibly be handled piecemeal; it cannot be cut up into fragments, but it must be considered in its entirety; or if for convenience it be subdivided, each portion must be considered in reference to every other portion and to the whole.

The student of anatomy necessarily cuts into fragments the human cadaver, but the most important, the most interesting organs — the heart, the lungs, the eyes — are to him but so much unmeaning and useless matter unless they are studied in connection with every other organ, and with the body as a whole. The story of the members of a man disputing about their relative importance well illustrates this point; each is essential as a part of the whole — all are useless or helpless when taken simply as parts.

It devolves upon a proponent to state his case and to prove it, and this I have sought to do. If, however, I have failed, the failure is owing to the feebleness of the individual rather than to the merits of the subject. But if not only the individual be incompetent, as well I may be in presence of such a theme, but the cause itself be wrong, or even impracticable in the end, my utmost efforts will of course be vain, and I will rejoice in failure, for I have no pride or vanity of any sort to exploit or sustain, and no selfish interest of any kind to subserve. But, right or wrong, a full and free discussion can never injure any good cause, for the maxim is that, when truth and error are free to contend, truth is sure finally to prevail. The individual may and doubtless will be injured in such conflict, but society itself will be the gainer.

But be this as it may, the great question of the prosperity of the South, and all that it implies, is now before the world, and it can be successfully met only by a broad and liberal discussion of the whole merits of the case. We cannot accept some points that are agreeable and reject others that are distasteful unless we can show that what is displeasing is repugnant, and what is pleasing is agreeable to reason itself.

We cannot say that God intends or God never intended so and so, because as yet none of us have been taken into the counsels of the Almighty.

We cannot say that the Negro is incapable of elevation because hitherto under surroundings which have always been adverse to improvement he has done little or nothing for the advancement of civilization and is still mostly a degraded savage or barbarian, because he has, when exposed to white influences, even those of servitude, greatly improved over his ancestors in Africa, and since freedom he has not only advanced as a race, but particularly as individuals, which we can see before our very eyes.

We cannot say that the South is a white man's country, and that therefore the whites must arbitrarily rule all other colors, even though they be free and equal citizens, for what makes it a white man's country? Does original possession? No; because we robbed the Indians of it and then exterminated them. Does nativity? Yes. Well, the Negroes were born here too, and therefore it is as much their country as ours. We cannot say that race prejudice forbids, for granting this kind of prejudice to be almost ineradicable, yet experience and a most elementary knowledge tell us that not only race but also religious prejudice, almost as ineradicable, has been immensely weakened and is still continually wearing away under the influence of reason and commercial intercourse. Humanity has solved many knotty and apparently insoluble questions, and race prejudice, like others, will be solved as well.

We cannot say such things *shall never* be, because can we ever expect to see in the future any greater changes than the present generation has witnessed — from the Negro a slave with his life practically in our hands to the Negro a lawmaker and a juryman sitting in judgment upon the property, yea, and upon the liberty, too, of the former master? and all with our acquiescence.

We cannot say we shall not amend this and cease to do that because others elsewhere do similar things, for this plea (it is not worthy of argument) is worthy only of wayward children, and it condones the reprehensible deeds of others.

We cannot say that the Negroes are wretched, poor, degraded, everything that is contemptible and objectionable, for that is but a stronger reason, from the standpoint of prosperity, why we should diligently seek to lift them up and render them thrifty and intelligent, for from nothing nothing can come, and from creatures in their present lowly, degraded and ineffective plight we can expect little or no assistance in our progress towards prosperity.

Yes, we can say and do all the things we ought not to do, and we can leave undone all the things we ought to do — all the power of the United States Government cannot compel us — but in following this course we are making an Ireland of the South, and are digging broad and deep graves in which to bury prosperity and all its untold advantages.

But enough; the idea is given, and now to the essay.

Richmond, Va., September, 1888

CHAPTER I

Prosperity not a free gift of Providence or Chance, but to be bought and full price paid — Is the South Prosperous?

Twenty-odd years ago, when I cast aside the sword and re-entered the walks of civil life, I fondly imagined a great era of prosperity for the South. Guided by history and by a knowledge of our people and our climatic and physical advantages, I saw in anticipation all her tribulations ended, all her scars healed, and all the ravages of war forgotten, and I beheld the South greater, richer and mightier than when she molded the political policy of the whole country. But year by year these hopes, chastened by experience, have waned and faded, until now, instead of beholding the glorious South of my imagination, I see her sons poorer than when war ceased his ravages, weaker than when rehabilitated with her original rights, and with the bitter memories of the past smoldering, if not rankling, in the bosoms of many.

And why all this great deviation from what was reasonable anticipation? Can it be that some wayward and malign providence, actuated by envy, hatred or malice, has guided our ways and efforts to disappointment and disaster, or has chance presided over and wrecked our destiny, or have there been causes of our own or of others', or of nature's, making, that have given us stones when we had reason to expect bread?

It cannot be providence, because we cannot suppose that providence is some fortuitous, arbitrary agent that can be swayed and swerved by prayers and supplications, or by threats and maledictions. Nor can we suppose that providence is a fickle dame, acting on one principle today and on the opposite one tomorrow, producing grapes from thorns one season, and figs from thistles the next. On the contrary, providence is strictly just, having no favorites, and holds the scales level between all creatures, regarding neither color, creed, previous condition, nor nationality. Providence is thoroughly realistic, and as thoroughly unsentimental, and smiles and frowns according to acts, and not according to intentions. Providence and justice are linked in close co-partnership, and if things turn not out according to our liking, we may be sure that we and not providence are at fault.

Nor can our disappointment be attributed to chance, blind or otherwise, for there is no such word as chance in religion, or modern philosophy either.

Then our disappointment, if disappointed we are, and our lack of prosperity, if unprosperous we be, must be due to cause. If to cause, then it behooves us to inquire honestly whether it be natural, and therefore irremediable, or artificial and of our own making, and therefore remediable by our own volition, or whether artificial but of others' making, and therefore remediable only by concert of action. If natural, and therefore beyond our control, we must accommodate ourselves thereto, for nature never consults man's convenience. If of our own making, and therefore remediable, it doubly behooves us to remove all such cause. But if of others' making, but yet remediable, it likewise behooves us to look around and seek for such removal too. Doubtless all these causes conspire more or less towards our lack of prosperity, but it is with the causes within our own control that we are now mainly concerned, and the others will not be touched.

The real question before us is: Is the South prosperous? If the correct answer be in the affirmative, then this proposed inquiry is altogether fruitless; but if in the negative, then this proposed inquiry into the prosperity of the South becomes the most momentous that can engage our attention. Judging by the glowing reports in the newspapers for the past three years, we must conclude that the South is enjoying a veritable deluge of prosperity, and that both individually and as states it is surpassing even the Eastern states, those petted children of legislation since the foundation of the Union. Judging by these sheets, one would naturally imagine that the South is a region where poverty is unknown and where everybody is industriously and successfully laying up wealth; where manufacturing sites are engrossing arable lands; where cotton, so long king, is tottering on his throne, and where manufactures are about to usurp his scepter. Seen through newspaper lenses, the South is indeed a happy Arcadia.

Just here it may be well to say a few words about so-called *Manufacturers' Records* which are circulating a vast amount of misinformation about the growth and prosperity of the South, and misleading multitudes on this point.

Such journals proceed on the same plan as would the Superintendent of the Census in 1890, should he, instead of actually enumerating the people, start with the population of 1880, and add thereto not only all the births, but also all the stillbirths, all the miscarriages, and all the abortions since that year, and deduct nothing for deaths in the meanwhile. Of course such a computation would be utterly absurd, and could only lead to ridiculous conclusions. But so it is with the computations of the so-called *Manufacturers' Records*. In arriving at their aggregates of additional manufactures they write to the proprietors of every scheme they see noticed in their local exchanges, and they include not only concerns that have actually begun operations, but also all projected and even all suggested enterprises, all of which they capitalize at the highest authorized amount; and to make their calculations all the more mischievous and misleading they deduct nothing for the many hundreds or many thousands of manufacturing concerns that annually fail or retire from business.

Thus in the census of 1880 the South is credited with $133,240,000 manufacturing capital, but for the last eight years these reliable records have, by including actual, probable, and possible manufacturing enterprises, by capitalizing them at their maximum and by deducting nothing for failures and retirements, added not less than $1,000,000,000 to the manufacturing capital of the South, or nearly eight times as much as the South started with in 1865 and had succeeded in gathering together during the subsequent fifteen years. The impression is sought to be conveyed that while the South had $133,240,000 employed in manufactures in 1880, she has in 1888 $1,133,240,000 so employed.* This is entirely false, because the South has lost since 1880 quite as much as she has gained in manufactures, or at the very best no one at all familiar with the South doubts that the census will show no greater increase of manufactures than it does population. The writer lives in one of the principal manufacturing cities of the South, and he observes therein no great increase of manufactures, the failures having almost if not quite offset the increase. In the mineral regions there has been some increase, but it is pretty certain that this growth has been fully offset by decadence in the South at large.

Newspaper compilations may discredit such opinions, but while such compilations are praiseworthy in intent, we all know what exaggerations they usually are when confronted by official documents. They are generally based upon "about" statements of the parties applied to, and in such cases "about" generally means largely in excess of the actual, just as current rumor reports A or B to be worth "about" one or ten millions, when the executor is glad to find half the "about." Thus in Richmond, the *Dispatch*'s compilation of manufactures for 1879 was $23,466,640, while according to the census of 1880, six months later, they were $20,790,000; and the population January 1, 1880, was 80,000 according to the board of health, while the census, taken five months later, gave a population of 63,600.

A few words also as to the glowing reports of the

* Thus the Baltimore *Manufacturers' Record* of March 29, 1889, reports for first quarter of 1889 an addition of $42,162,000 to the manufacturing capital of the eleven Southern states.

prosperity of the South as set forth by Colonel Alex. K. McClure,[1] Hon. Wm. D. Kelley,[2] and others. These gentlemen occupy pretty much the position of kings who, surrounded by ministers and courtiers whose interest it is to keep them in darkness, rarely if ever know the true state of affairs, and their opinions are of as little value. These gentlemen who undertake to learn the condition of affairs by a hurried trip in palace cars are usually taken in charge and coached by interested parties, who carry them to a few se-lected spots like Birmingham and Chattanooga, where there is much life, activity and growth, and are told exultingly, "There! Look! Does not this remind you of Pennsylvania?" etc., etc. These gentlemen are thus placed in the attitude of envoys in olden times to an enemy's camp. The envoys were led blindfolded through the camp, and their eyes were unbandaged only when they reached the royal headquarters, where everything had been prearranged to impress them with the power and magnificence of the army or sovereign. So these gentlemen, having been hurried through hundreds of miles in luxurious palace coaches, have practically been blindfolded as to the condition of the country passed through, and not having their eyes unbandaged until in the midst of furnaces, roll-ing mills, and all the activities of a manufacturing cen-ter, they are dazzled by what they see, and they at once jump to the conclusion that what they behold is merely a type of the whole South, and that as there

[1] Alexander K. McClure, *The South: Its Industrial, Financial and Political Condition* (Philadelphia, 1886). (ED.)

[2] William D. Kelley, *The Old South and the New* (New York, 1888). (ED.)

is great prosperity before their eyes, so there is great prosperity in the South.

These gentlemen altogether forget, most likely, listening to the brilliant conversation of their chaperons about the new South — have not seen the hundreds and hundreds of miles of poor country passed through, with its fenceless plantations, its unpainted and dilapidated homesteads, its small proportion of cultivated fields and its large proportion of lands returning and returned to a state of nature, its patches instead of its fields of crops, the scarcity of stock of all kinds, and the thriftless and idle groups found at almost every depot. They lose sight of the real South — that is to say, of ninety-five per cent thereof, but seeing the other five per cent concentrated in two or three active, stirring, and busy cities they erroneously conclude that the ninety-five per cent which they do not and cannot see is like the five per cent which they have been invited to inspect. Reversing the process of the tiny fragment held close to the eye hiding the sun, and holding these bits of sunshine close to the eye, the South at large, great though its poverty actually is, is made to appear as bright and as prosperous as these bits of sunshine.

If, instead of this process, these gentlemen would visit the farming and planting community, whether cotton, tobacco, sugar, grain, or whatnot be raised, which is the real South, and if they were brought into actual business contact with the people themselves, they would soon see, even leaving out the six millions of Negroes who are in the depths of indigence, that fully ninety-five per cent of the whites would at death leave their families, after debts were paid, with scarcely more than a roof to cover them, and that for every ten living in any degree of ease and comfort there were ninety who had nothing beyond the commonest necessaries of life. Yes, there shall be a new South, and prominent men from the North must be brought to testify to it, even though their testimony must in the nature of the case be untrustworthy and valueless.

To doubt is to be damned, is true in other things besides religion, and so to doubt the current charming presentations of Southern growth and prosperity is to bring down anathemas upon one's head. What! the South not prosperous? Impossible, they cry; and the individual who questions is an idiot.

Would that the South were rich, because numberless blessings follow in the train of wealth, just as numberless evils follow in the trail of poverty. To be rich is to be great, mighty and powerful, to be feared, honored and respected, like the United States, like Great Britain, like Germany; to be poor is to be weak, wretched and miserable, to be despised, plundered and imposed upon, like Spain, Turkey, or Mexico. If claiming to be rich could make the South rich, none could make louder or more vehement claims than myself, and a rejuvenated giant South should ever be on my tongue; but claims and boasts are vain in the face of nature, which demands deeds and not sentiments, but deeds in accordance with principles of well-established economic laws.

Prosperity is an inestimable blessing, and to obtain it we must, like the husbandman in Scripture who sold everything to purchase one field, make every sacrifice, and be deterred by no difficulties; but like all other good things prosperity has its price, and we must pay the full price or must go without, and the greater the good the greater the cost. We all desire prosperity, and we have been sighing for it for years, and yet prosperity lags; but if we have it not it is because we have not sought aright — that is, not in accordance with the laws of nature.

In order for success one must understand fully his position as well as be willing to take all necessary steps to secure success, for his measures cannot be appropriate if this knowledge be lacking.

So in the following pages I will, in order to do my mite towards placing the South in the proud and influential position she should occupy, endeavor to set forth, first, her actual condition and conspiring causes; and second, I will seek to point out the steps necessary to be taken in order to attain prosperity. In doing the first, I will not draw for facts upon irresponsible newspapers, but upon United States official documents, mainly those of the census of 1880, or upon other sources which are universally recognized as authorities. The principal cause thereof — namely, the degradation of the Negro — will be set forth at length, but candidly and plainly, so that if possible others may see as I do, or so that the resulting discussion may clear my vision and that of others seeing as I do.

In doing the second, the remedies will require greater space, but they will be treated in the same plain, candid and fair manner as in discussing the condition and cause thereof of the South; and all will be done solely with a view to letting us see ourselves as we really are, so that perceiving clearly what is essential to be done, and being willing to do it, we may attain our longed-for prosperity, the one thing needful for our happiness as individuals, and for our greatness as states.

CHAPTER II

South not Prosperous — Why? — Principal Cause Degradation of the Negro — Elevation of the Negro Urged on Economic Grounds, not on Grounds of Justice or Religion.

As many streams are required to make the river, so many causes are required to produce prosperity, and as the river is great in proportion to the number of streams flowing together, so prosperity is great in proportion to the number of causes harmoniously co-operating.

There are many causes conspiring to the poverty or lack of prosperity of the South, the principal of which are a general prevalence of ignorance, a general disregard of human life, a general lack of economy and self-denial; but great as these causes are, a greater and more far-reaching cause of all is the degradation of the Negro, who, being our principal source of labor, is our principal dependence for prosperity.

Each of these causes would greatly retard the prosperity of the South, or indeed of any country, but all of them combined, destructive as they would necessarily be to prosperity, are not as serious and as fatal as the last cause, namely: the degradation of the

Negro. Like a malignant cancer which poisons the whole system, this degradation seems to intensify all the other drawbacks under which we labor. Thus general ignorance is intensified by the gross ignorance of all the blacks and of the whites nearest them in social and financial condition; the general disregard of human life is intensified by the slight regard in which a Negro's life is held, and the whites, regarding the Negro's life of little sanctity, naturally regard all life as of little value, and therefore freely take each other's life; and the general lack of economy and self-denial is naturally intensified by the careless, wasteful and negligent manner in which the Negro, upon whom we are mainly dependent for labor, usually does his work. The Negro is an extremely defective tool, and no man, whether planter, carpenter, or whatnot, can continue constantly to use wretched implements without becoming wasteful and negligent himself, and without disregarding economy. We may remove all the other hindrances to prosperity; the whites may become well educated; we may hold human life in scrupulous regard and may become models of economy and self-denial, but if the blacks are to be left to grovel in their present degraded condition, even then prosperity would be measurably in default, because the six million Negroes, remaining degraded, would prove an incubus upon the whites, who would be in imminent danger of impoverishment by the thieving of such multitudes, whose highest and only ambition would be to live without work at the expense of those who were responsible for their degradation. But then let education be generally disseminated among the whites as it is in some of the other states, let human life be as well protected as in a really civilized community — England, for example — and let economy and self-denial prevail as in the New England states; the elevation of the Negro would follow as a matter of course, or rather it would go along *pari passu* with the elevation of the whites themselves, and his degradation as a race would become a matter of history.

Although justice — and we should always bear in mind that justice is a stern virtue that will sooner or later avenge herself upon her violators, though at the same time she never fails to honor and reward those who respect her requirements — although justice demands that the whites elevate the Negroes, for in the light of morality we stand responsible for their welfare, their elevation will not be advocated on any such ground, nor on the ground of religion either, but simply on economic grounds, on the ground of advantage to the whites. Just as we would urge the South to improve its animals, tools, methods of planting, etc., so that it may derive the more good from their labor and capital, so we urge the elevation of the Negroes, because the better men and citizens they are the more we, the whites, can in the end make out of them.

That is very hard doctrine, perhaps, but we must remember that facts themselves are hard things, and that they never think of accommodating themselves to either our desires or our fancies. We would like a more "comforting" (as the women would say) doctrine, did not reading, observation and experience show that morality and even religion are very poor advocates, unless they can show to their listeners that material benefit is on their side. Convinced, therefore, as I must be that benefit is the only safe and sound ground to base an argument upon (for if a thing does not benefit or afford us pleasure in some way, how can it interest us?) I shall address all my arguments to prove not only that the prosperity of the South will be increased by, but that it is dependent upon, the elevation of the Negro, and if it is not so shown, then this effort will be in vain, and if it cannot be so shown, then all effort to elevate the Negro will be in vain. If the Southern people cannot be shown that his elevation is for their interest, then the Negro must forever grovel, but if it is demonstrated as we go along that his elevation is essential to our welfare, then as sensible people we should throw aside the thickly encrusted prepossessions or prejudices of centuries and hasten the day when we shall have made the Negro a free man (for as long as he labors under any but natural disabilities he is little better than a serf), and therefore a worthy and competent co-worker in the race for prosperity, which we have long seen through a glass darkly, but which, like an *ignis fatuus*, has eluded our grasp, and which will continue to as long as the Negro is degraded and without hope of rising above his present status — a status of perpetual inferiority and subordination.

In discussing this question, which is the gravest and most momentous confronting the South, now happily mostly local, but which before long will become national if the South proves herself incapable or unwilling to solve it, I shall set forth, first, the material condition of the South, drawn from well-established sources, which will be seen to be one of great poverty

— certainly of comparative poverty; and, second, after showing the state of education I will point out at greater length the steps which are necessary to convert, by elevating the Negro, this poverty into prosperity.

It may seem both invidious and presumptuous to attempt this role, but while frankly admitting that I may be presumptuous, my Southern ancestry, birth, rearing, residence and interest preserve me from the charge of invidiousness; but if my directing attention to the poverty and illiteracy of the South be thought by many to be unpatriotic, or if my opposition to our present undemocratic condition of affairs be considered treasonable, I will then patiently bear the odium attached to such charges.

CHAPTER III

South not Prosperous — Example of Georgia — Her Poverty — Contrary Example of Palatinate in 1674 — Few or no Savings Banks — Few other Banks — Proportion of Railways — Very Few Manufactures and they very Crude — Statistics Thereof — Production of Iron and Steel in 1887 — Manufactures of Thirteen Southern Cities — Summary of Aggregated Wealth.

That the South ought to be the richest section of the United States goes without saying, for it occupies not only a broad and fertile territory, but it lies beneath a sun that produces in abundance many of the most valuable productions of commerce. In addition to the great staff of life — bread — tobacco and cotton flourish here as nowhere else, and rice, sugar, and naval stores add millions annually to its wealth; but although this production has been going on uninterruptedly for more than twenty years her people are not rich, but on the contary are very poor. They are not only burdened with debt up to their full capacity for borrowing, but much, if not the greatest part, of their crops is made by loans, beginning with the time of planting. Their homes are not only unsupplied with many of the most essential comforts, but their plantations are ill supplied with stock and implements, their cribs and smokehouses are mostly empty, their fences have disappeared, and their dwellings and farm buildings are not only indifferent, but they present a general appearance of neglect and too often of dilapidation. The want of accumulated capital is extreme, and for at least six months of the year money, instead of being a reality, is rather a thing of memory and of hope, or of the past and the future, with the greater part of the people. But as an ounce of prevention is worth a pound of cure, so well-attested facts, even though they be few, are worth libraries of speculations and assertion. We will therefore bid adieu to assertions which are of no authority, and will resort to facts to substantiate our statements.

We have all heard of Georgia, of her great progress and prosperity; and as she has been held up as a model to all the other states, we of the South have come to recognize her authority on both material and moral matters with the utmost reverence and humility; we can therefore all rely upon what Georgia does and says. We will, then, refer to Georgia, and trust what she says regarding the material condition of her people, and her Comptroller-General, in his annual report for the year ending September 30, 1886, shall be the spokesman.

But before proceeding to the analysis of this report, let us remark that it was made twenty years after the close of the war, in which Georgia was not especially scourged except along the line of Sherman's march. Let us also remark that Turenne[1] in 1674 devastated the Palatinate to such a degree that in the language of General Sheridan "a crow flying across it was compelled to carry his rations," even the fruit trees and the vines being destroyed, yet twenty years thereafter scarcely a trace of her horrible devastation was visible. Now, bearing further in mind that this report was made twenty years after the war, we will expect to find that Georgia had repaired her ravages quite as well as had the pauper labor of the Palatinate. According to the report, we find the following condition of wealth:

Assessed value of personal property			$123,141,286.00
"	"	per capita, adding 15 per cent increase from 1880 to 1886	70.00
"	"	per capita — whites	124.47
"	"	" " — Negroes	6.54
"	"	whites — household and kitchen furniture	12.30
"	"	Negroes — household and kitchen furniture	1.03
"	"	whites — plantation and mechanical tools	5.65
"	"	Negroes — plantation and mechanical tools	.31
"	"	whites — livestock all kinds .	24.58
"	"	Negroes — livestock all kinds	2.60

Personal property is taken because real estate remaining substantially the same is not, in agricultural communities, subject to much change of value.

Now reflect for a moment. Here are people labor-

---

[1] Vicomte Henri de la Tour d'Auvergne de Turenne (1611-1675). (Ed.)

ing for twenty years, and granted they began with *no*
personal property, they have gathered wealth at the
annual rate per head of $3.50, or at the rate of $6.18
for the whites; and counting a family of five per-
sons, each family has accumulated annually $17.50, or
$30.90 for each white family. But this is on the sup-
position that everybody started as they came into the
world — with not a rag to their back, with not a chair,
table or bed, with not a pan, plate or dish, with not a
wagon, plow or hoe, with not a horse, cow or hog —
in fact, with nothing. But as it is scarcely possible to
conceive of a respectable white family without at least
$61.50 of household and kitchen furniture, or of a
plantation without at least $28.25 of implements and
tools, or without $123 of livestock of all kinds, one
fairly good mule being worth that, it is not unreason-
able to affirm that the people of Georgia had not
added materially to their wealth during the twenty
years preceding 1886.

But it has been claimed that the Negroes of Georgia
have also prospered very much. What does the report
say? The Negroes at least began with no accumulated
property. According to the report each colored family
possessed in 1886 an average of $5.15 of household and
kitchen furniture, of $1.55 of mechanical and farming
implements, and of $13 of livestock of all kinds.

Truly prosperity ran riot with the colored brother,
and, since he is so wealthy, it is not surprising that we
have the pretty general complaint that the Negro is
lazy and won't work.

If we find no prosperity in Georgia it will be vain
to look for it in the other Southern states, and we will
not, therefore, adduce any more statistics, although

they are to hand in abundance. But granting prosperity for the whites, who can deny that the blacks, who comprise forty per cent of the population, are in the very depths of poverty, and therefore of degradation, for poverty and degradation are always twin sisters; and that if anything has been done to elevate them the attempt has been a lamentable failure. Leaving now individual let us come to general or aggregate wealth, a few particulars of which must, for want of space, suffice. And first — savings banks.

In settled countries where the land has been cleared, fences made and houses built, if there is any, certainly if there is much prosperity, money will accumulate, and it will find its way into savings banks, and cause their formation if there are none or not enough already exist. In new states like Florida, Texas and Arkansas, savings banks may not be expected, because prosperous people can find better uses for their money in buying lands and opening new farms than in putting it in savings banks. But in the other eight Southern states, where land is all appropriated, the accumulations that follow thrift would almost certainly find their way into savings banks, and if savings banks do not appear and flourish, it may be accepted as infallible evidence that there is little or no prosperity. Now what do we find?

The United States Comptroller of the Treasury in his report for 1885-86 reports:

	Deposits in savings banks
Southern states	....
All other states	$1,141,530,578.00

There were doubtless some few savings banks in the South, but none to attract the attention of an official who is himself a Southerner.

Banks are another evidence of prosperity, for the accumulations of prosperity naturally seek investment in banks. The following is the report of the United States Comptroller of the Currency, December 4, 1886:

	Southern States	Other States
Capital stock paid in	$31,065,450.00	$517,175,280.00
Surplus fund	8,262,139.00	148,987,051.00
Undivided profits	4,483,274.00	62,020,200.00
Total	$43,810,863.00	$728,182,531.00

Banks are not only evidences of prosperity, but they are in turn causes of prosperity. What shall we say, then, of the prosperity of the South when it possesses six per cent of banking capital for twenty-six per cent of population?

Railroads are also an index of wealth, and what is their testimony? The highest authority (Poor's R. R. Manual for 1886) reports:

	Southern states	Other states
Total investments	$1,108,428,000	$7,230,858,000

This is a better showing than in savings banks and banks, for it is thirteen per cent to twenty-six per cent of population. But this showing is delusive, because it is well known that almost all Southern roads have been built with Northern capital, and that not five per cent of the total of $1,108,428,000 is owned in the South. Except as occupying Southern soil and as sources of taxation, railroads are scarcely more Southern in origin and ownership than if they were located in one of the planets.

Manufactures are other evidences of wealth, and what is their report? Here we have to go back some years to the United States census of 1880, but this evidence will probably be demurred to by devout believers in a new South, for they will say manufactures have made wonderful strides since then. Such objectors may be correct, but it is extremely doubtful, because except in Birmingham, Chattanooga and a few other localities an observer can behold few material evidences of increase of manufactures; certainly nothing commensurate with the growth of manufactures in most of the other states. The last census reports: manufactures in the South, $240,444,295; in all other, $5,129,223,411; which is not quite five per cent, against twenty-six per cent of population. Bearing in mind that Southern manufactures were mostly of the coarsest character, requiring the least skill and therefore earning the least profit, the poverty of the South under this head is all the more striking and lamentable; and to show this, the following digest is made from the report:

ELEVEN SOUTHERN STATES

Cotton manufactures	16,165,607
Woolen manufactures	2,336,597
Flour and grist mills	63,803,041
Foundry products	7,091,959
Iron and steel products	7,836,653
Lumber products	31,620,878
Naval stores	5,871,983
Tobacco	20,138,340
	$154,865,058

Observe that $63,803,041 is credited to flour and grist mills, which are mostly small neighborhood affairs, and most of this amount is as fairly credited to manufactures as if we credited to bakeries the subsequent labors of the women in converting the flour and the meal into loaf-bread, biscuits, ashcake and pone. To the credit of lumber is passed $31,620,878. This is one of the crudest of manufactures, and instead of classing sawmills under the head of wealth-producers, we should rather class them under the head of bankruptcy-breeders. Only $18,502,204 goes to the credit of textiles, and only $14,928,612 to iron and steel and their varied products.

The difference, according to the census, between cost of manufactures and what the manufactures sell for is twenty per cent. Therefore, in the census year seventy-four per cent of population added about $1,000,000,000 to their wealth, while the twenty-six per cent of Southern population added only $48,000,-000.

This was in 1880, and probably we may hear a chorus of "patriotic" Southerners and enthusiastic believers in a new South scornfully exclaim, "1880! oh, yes, 1880!" and most probably these gentlemen will exclaim, "Talk at this stage of the world, when the South is taking such giant strides, of 1880; you had as well talk to us about the time when Captain John Smith was having his romantic adventure with old Powhatan and his lovely Pocahontas."

But although we have no late census to refer to, we have official figures of the iron industry, the one in which the South is said to have accomplished most, so let us see what these figures say:

	1880		
	South	Whole country	Percentage
	Tons	Tons	South
Production pig iron	207,798	4,295,414	5
	1887		
Production pig iron	767,791	7,187,206	10
Production steel, all kinds		3,739,760	0

Here is a wonderful progress, worthy of being celebrated with a full band of Jew's harps. Here is the South with enough coal and iron, almost locked in each other's embrace, to supply the world with iron at the very lowest cost, and yet in seven years she has added 560,000 tons to her product, or an additional five per cent on the total production of the whole country. While the South was adding 560,000 tons the rest of the country added 2,900,000 tons. Observe that the South is not credited with a pound of the 3,739,760 tons of steel produced in 1887.

The census of 1880 gives in minute detail the manufactures of over one hundred principal cities and the following summary is presented: Thirteen Southern cities, total manufactures, $77,191,000, of which

Richmond manufactured		$ 20,790,000
New Orleans	"	18,808,000
Nashville	"	8,597,000
Atlanta	"	4,862,000
Memphis	"	4,413,000

As a comparison the following is interesting:

New York manufactured		$472,926,000
Philadelphia	"	324,345,000
Chicago	"	249,023,000
Brooklyn	"	177,220,000
Boston	"	130,532,000
St. Louis	"	114,333,000
Cincinnati	"	105,259,000
Pittsburgh	"	75,915,000

It will be observed that New York City manufactured about twice as much as the whole South, and Chicago as much, and when the grade of manufactures of the two sections is considered, the comparison will be all the more striking. Note, also, that Pittsburgh manufactured nearly as much as thirteen principal Southern cities.

"Patriotism" would say hide all these uncomplimentary facts, but common sense says it is better to look our deficiencies squarely in the face, for we will never overcome our shortcomings until we are convinced of their existence. Common sense beats "patriotism" every time, and while things frequently go backwards under the lead of "patriotism," which is only a longer word for "gush," they are always pushing forward under the guidance of common sense. "Know thyself" is not only essential for the individual, but also for the state.

At the close of this branch of our subject we condense our facts into a summary, so that we may see our condition at a glance.

EXHIBIT OF AGGREGATE WEALTH

Value per head personal property in Georgia		$70.00
" " for whites	$124.47	
" " for blacks	6.54	

Value per head household and kitchen furniture, whites .. 12.30
"   "   "   "   "   "   blacks .. 1.03
"   "   farm and mechanical tools, whites 5.65
"   "   "   "   "   "   blacks .... .31
"   "   livestocks, all kinds, whites 24.58
"   "   "   "   "   blacks 2.60

EXHIBIT OF INDIVIDUAL WEALTH

Sources	South	Other states	Per cent of Southern population	Per cent South
Savings banks	....	1,141,530,578	26	..
National banks	43,810,863	728,182,531	26	6
State b'ks. and bank'rs. ...	very little	nearly all	26	trace
Telegraph stock	nothing	all	26	..
L. F. & M. insurance stocks	very little	nearly all	26	trace
Vessel property	very little	nearly all	26	trace
Manufactures, 1880	240,444,295	5,129,223,411	26	5
Pig iron, 1880 — tons	207,798	4,087,616	26	5
Pig iron, 1887 — tons	767,791	6,419,415	26	10
Steel, 1887 — tons	....	3,739,760	26	..
Railroads	1,108,428,000	7,230,858,000	26	13

CHAPTER IV

Growth of Cities and Causes Thereof — Examples — Growth of Thirty Southern Cities and of Four Ohio and Four New Jersey Cities.

But the optimists, though staggered probably by the preceding unfavorable statistics, will, in proof of their claim of the great progress and prosperity of the South, point triumphantly to the growth of the cities.

Well, granting all claimed, what does it amount to, unless it can be shown that the growth of the cities is the outgrowth of the prosperity of the farming and rural districts, for it by no means follows that growth of cities always means the prosperity of the state? Generally, perhaps, growth of cities means prosperity of the state, but sometimes it means decay. In the case of England and Scotland their fifty-three cities, ranging in population by census of 1881 from 50,762 to 3,832,441, means prosperity, but the twenty-four cities of Italy (census 1881), ranging in population from 50,651 to 494,314, and the fifteen cities of Spain (census 1877), ranging from 49,855 to 397,690, does not mean either prosperity or progress, for both Italy and Spain are extremely poor, backward and stagnant.

There are other causes than prosperity to promote the growth of cities. Decay also promotes their growth, or at least temporarily, and cities sometimes linger long after the country is dead. Constantinople was a populous city long after the Eastern Empire was a mere shadow, and Constantinople is still a populous city, although the Ottoman Empire has been moribund the last one hundred years.

In a declining or decaying state, with agriculture on the wane and social order disturbed, there is a constant influx into the cities — where there is more life and activity, more society, and especially more security. In such a state, the younger and more ambitious desert the villages and the country because they have a lessening field for their energies; professional men of all kinds do the same; families of means and culture, tiring of a country life constantly becoming harder and more unsocial, follow next; then follow the timid, who dread the relaxations of legal restraint upon the improvident and badly disposed, and then those seeking the advantages of education, which constantly diminish in such a state. And along with what may be termed the higher classes, the mechanical and laboring people, who find work becoming scarcer and wages smaller and more uncertain, also flock to the cities, where, if anywhere, employment is to be had. And thus it is that cities grow in decaying countries.

Now, most of these causes of increase of our cities have been operating for the past twenty years, and they have not yet exhausted their forces. Thousands and tens of thousands, yea hundreds of thousands, of our most cultured and refined people have deserted their ancestral homes and have settled in Southern cities and elsewhere in the United States, and few or none have taken their places. The writer knows of neighborhoods that have been deserted almost *en masse* by their former wealthy inhabitants, and plantations, where twenty years ago Negroes were to be found by the fourscore, are now almost tenantless wastes. And let any city resident of twenty years' standing inquire who his neighbors and acquaintances are, and he will be astonished at the numbers who have within that time from some one of the foregoing causes emigrated from the country; and let any householder inquire into the origin of the servants he employs, and he will find that fully half are country-bred. But the city's gain has been the country's loss, for few have taken the places of those who have turned their backs upon their birthplaces and family burying grounds.

But have our cities really increased much in population? Let us see. But, unfortunately, in order to do so, we must go back to antiquity — namely, the census of 1880 — for this authority will be repudiated by the optimists of these modern days, to wit: the year of grace, 1888. They will claim enormous gains since 1880, and they are doubtless correct as to a considerable increase in many instances; but when we remember how easy it is to make claims when no proof is demanded, or when no disproof is ready at hand, we should not be surprised at the great claims of increase that every city makes, and discount them accordingly. There is among the denizens of every city — and we might say of every village, too — a sense of personal responsibility for the growth of such place; there is a feeling of pride if the place is thought to be growing, and of mortification if it is thought to be stationary, or even growing slowly, and in order to nourish their pride and to conceal their mortification, they all naturally fall into the habit of exaggerating the growth of their city, town, or village. If the place of their residence is found by accurate census to have grown and to be still growing rapidly, so that it outstrips other cities that they had been jealous of, then a regular *civis Romanus sum* feeling takes possession of them, and they brag, and strut, and bluster, as if they had performed some great deeds. Who does not remember the general dissatisfaction with the last census when it failed to show such growth as localities and cities had fondly claimed?

But here is what the census of 1880 says as to the growth of the thirty principal Southern cities:

	Population in 1880	Increase 1870 to 1880
Alexandria	13,659	89
Atlanta	37,409	15,620
Augusta	21,891	6,502
Chattanooga	12,892	6,799
Charleston	49,984	1,028
Columbus, Ga.	10,123	2,722
Columbia	10,036	738
Galveston	22,248	8,430
Greenville, S. C.	6,160	2,409
Jackson, Miss.	5,204	970
Jacksonville	7,650	738
Knoxville	9,633	1,013
Little Rock	13,108	758
Lynchburg	15,959	9,134
Macon	12,749	1,939
Montgomery	16,713	6,125
Nashville	43,350	17,485
New Orleans	216,090	24,672
Norfolk	21,966	2,737

Petersburg	21,656	2,706
Portsmouth	13,390	800
Richmond	63,600	12,562
Raleigh	9,265	1,475
Savannah	30,709	2,474
San Antonio	20,550	8,430
Wilmington, N. C.	17,350	3,904
Total		142,259

From which deduct the decrease in the following cities during the same decade —

Memphis	33,592	6,634
Mobile	29,132	2,902
Natchez	7,058	1,999
Vicksburg	11,814	629
Total		12,164

— and we have a net increase in the growth of the thirty principal Southern cities of 130,095.

Compare this growth with that of the four Ohio cities:

	Increase 1870 to 1880
Cincinnati	38,900
Columbus	20,373
Cleveland	67,316
Toledo	18,533
	145,122

or with that of the four Jersey cities:

Camden	21,604
Jersey City	38,176
Newark	47,929
Paterson	29,694
	137,403

In view of these *facts*, will it not seem amusing to speak of the growth and prosperity of the South? And even this increase is partially delusive, because the census of 1870 was taken when political affairs were very much out of joint, when the work was committed to ignorant and careless hands, and was therefore very imperfectly done.

CHAPTER V

Why Elevate the Negro? To make Him an Efficient and Profitable Wealth-Producer — — Must Trample or Must Elevate — Must make Him a Slave or a Man — Labor Cornerstone of Wealth. Examples of No-Worker, of Unintelligent Worker, and of Intelligent Worker — South can expect Prosperity only through Intelligent Labor — United States would still be a Wilderness but for Intelligent Labor.

Having sufficiently demonstrated, it is thought, not only the comparative, but also the positive, poverty of the South, which ought in many respects to be the richest section, let us now proceed to point out some of the causes of this poverty, or at all events of this want of prosperity.

As already stated, these causes are many, the chief of which are illiteracy, disregard of human life, lack of economy and self-denial, and degradation of the Negro — already mentioned — and vicious economic legislation, one of the most insidious, because generally unsuspected, of all the causes sapping our prosperity.

For want of space only one of these causes will be treated, except incidentally, but as this cause is the greatest of all, and in a measure underlies all but the last cause, by handling this cause properly, the whole field affecting our prosperity will have been gone over. This cause is the degradation of the Negro.

But the question really to be considered is not the degradation of the Negro, for that is patent to all, but the elevation of the Negro, since it is by his elevation alone that we are to secure prosperity; for elevate him and the other evils will be cured during the process of his elevation.

But the question will be very generally asked, Why elevate the Negro at all? Is he not now good enough to obey us obsequiously, and to make our corn, our cotton, our tobacco, our rice, and our sugar? What more do we want of him? The reply is that if the Negro is forever to remain simply the instrument for doing our menial and manual work, for plowing and sowing, for driving mules, for worming tobacco and picking cotton, he is already too elevated, and he should be still further humbled and degraded. In his present condition he has some of the ideas and aspirations of a freeman, some desires for education, and he has almost entire control of his personal movements. He works when it suits him, but then he may idle at the crisis of a crop; but as we cannot compel him with the lash to work, he is on the whole not a profitable laborer either for himself or for an employer. To make him efficient, and to make him work the crop at the proper time, in spite of the attractions of political and religious gatherings, the overseer with the lash must be ever before his eyes. To allow the Negro to remain as he is, is for him a still "lower deep" in the social scale, and in his descent he drags us down with him.

But if the Negro is to become an intelligent voter, is to be a citizen capable of taking a sensible part in the affairs of his community, and to be a valuable co-worker in adding to the wealth of the State, then we have a vast deal to do in order to elevate him. To make him *our* assistant in the production of wealth, the Negro must be made to work, or he must be induced by ambition, by the hope of enjoying in full the fruits of his labors, to work steadily and intelligently. If we are not willing to elevate him, we should set to work resolutely and deliberately to manacle both his mind and limbs, and to cow him, so that a little white child shall control a thousand. We will then at least get enough out of him to supply his few physical wants and to enable us to live in idleness and comparative comfort, which is not now the case. But if there is no hope of our ever being able to do this, what is the next best thing for us to do for our own good? Make a man of him. But this can be done only by means of education and other fostering influences, by cultivating his self-respect, by inspiring his hope, by letting him see that the land of his birth is as much his country as it is that of the wealthiest and haughtiest white. Now he is not only an alien, but an inferior — in reality a serf, in the land of his nativity.

We must trample, or we must elevate; to maintain the *status quo* is impossible. To trample is to perpetuate and intensify the poverty and stagnation under which we groan; to elevate is to make the South rich, happy and strong.

To say that labor is the cornerstone — yea, the

whole foundation, too, of wealth — is merely to utter a truism, but how few of us, while freely acknowledging, actually realize this fact. For example: Place a man and his family in a Garden of Eden, where fruits, ripening the year round, abound on every hand, and where the climate requires slight clothing and shelter, and suppose none of them labors. If they had been supplied with tools, house and garments, in a few years at furthest they would be naked, toolless and houseless, for these things wear out or decay; or if they had not been supplied with these things they would, not laboring, at the end of ten, fifty or a thousand years be the same helpless, useless animals they were when first created.

But suppose the members of this family willing to work and anxious to improve their condition, but suppose through ignorance they do not know how to avail themselves of the forces of nature, or suppose they misapplied the little knowledge they did gain through painful experience; at the end of ten, fifty or a thousand years they would not be greatly better off, and though increased in numbers, the family would most probably be like and no further advanced than were the Indians when our ancestors landed and began to rob them of their homes and patrimony. This family was industrious, but not intelligent.

But suppose these same people not only willing to work and anxious to improve their condition, but intelligent also, inquisitive of nature, and availing themselves of the forces of air and water in their various applications, and prying into the laws of mechanics and inventing weapons, tools, vehicles, etc., etc.; then at the end of twenty years this family will have made considerable advance in its condition; at the end of a century or two it will have grown into a barbarous tribe of some size and importance; and at the end of a millennium it will have developed into a wealthy and powerful kingdom.

By this simple, though perhaps needless illustration, we may clearly see that not merely labor, but intelligent labor, is the sole basis of prosperity, and that prosperity is proportionate to the intelligence of labor. This is, however, merely preliminary to saying that the South is no exception to this universal truth, and that she, like all other countries, can expect prosperity only in proportion to the intelligence of her laborers. And by intelligence is not meant simply book-learning, for frequently those deeply versed in books are learned, but they are far from being intelligent; but by intelligence is meant a certain alertness of perception which enables one to grasp the situation or business in hand so as to avoid the difficulties or hindrances presented, and to appropriate the advantages offered. And by laborers is not meant simply those who dig and plow and who do the manual work of society, but also those who think, plan and direct.

Thus the first agriculturists, being ignorant, could devise no better aid than a sharp, hard stick for stirring the soil, but, intelligence aiding, they followed this with a spade made of the shoulder-blade of some wild beast; this was followed by a forked limb drawn by a domestic animal. But intelligence has not ceased her efforts, although science and skill seem to have reached perfection in the modern plow. And this same holds true with spinning, weaving, sewing, locomotion, etc., etc. — in almost everything, intelligent labor has, as it were, evolved the mighty oak out of the tiny acorn. Intelligent labor has converted the Western wilderness into great and populous states, to which the scepter of empire is being fast transferred; and labor lacking in intelligence has left the South, with all her great advantages of soil and climate, far in the rear of states born but yesterday. But for intelligence mingling with and directing labor, the world would yet be in its barbarous and savage infancy, and there would be no Gladstone to depict its youth, and the United States, instead of being peopled by sixty millions of the happiest human beings, would yet be the heritage of cruel tribes numbering less perhaps than the population of our chiefest city.

Education and intelligence do not always go hand in hand in the individual, but education is the parent of intelligence as intelligence is the parent of prosperity.

CHAPTER VI

Prosperity in Proportion to Intelligence — Illiteracy in Southern, Western, and New England States — Ignorance is Poverty and Degradation for Whites and Blacks Alike — Poverty will Continue as long as Ignorance — Prosperity of the South Bound up with Elevation of the Laboring Population.

All then being agreed that intelligent labor is the basis of prosperity, may it not be fairly claimed that if a country otherwise favorably situated is not prosperous, it must be because its labor is not intelligent — and by labor is meant not merely those who drive the plow and swing the scythe, who handle the saw and push the plane, who ply the trowel and wield the hammer, but all who guide, plan and command: in a word, all who aid by hand or head in the production of wealth? And not only will all agree that intelligence is the parent of prosperity, but all will likewise agree that Negro labor, which is our principal dependence, is extremely deficient in both education and intelligence. But while all may not agree that the white labor of the South is greatly lacking in intelligence and efficiency, yet those who are acquainted with white labor in the South and elsewhere will agree that even our white labor is inferior to similar labor elsewhere. The simple fact that (census 1880) 3,254,106 Southerners out of a total of 8,827,676 of the age of ten and upwards could not read, is strong evidence of lack of general intelligence. While in the eight Western states, from Michigan to Kansas, the proportion of illiterates is 413,547 to 10,785,090, in the six New England states it is 157,233 to 3,219,856, and in the three Middle states it is 351,899 to 8,050,634. This exhibit of itself may very well explain the great difference in prosperity and progress between South and North; and who can question that the South would be infinitely greater, wealthier and happier if her people were educated to the same extent as are the people of the North and West?

If, as heretofore claimed, there are causes for the absence of prosperity in the South, as already partially set forth, may not the principal cause be attributed to the lack of education and consequent inefficiency and degradation of our laboring population? That lack of education to the extent we see prevalent in the South is the parent of inefficiency and degradation, is a proposition needing no demonstration, for education means brightening and sharpening man's mental faculties, purifying his morals and manners, and refining his tastes. The individual devoid of education is little above the plane of the brutes, and in some respects he is worse; for he has vices and passions the brute is a stranger to, and he exercises little or no restraint in their indulgence. Such a person is satisfied with life in its lowest phases, and as long as he has enough, regardless of kind or quality, to fill the belly, he has little or no desire to improve his degraded lot. This applies to whites as well as to blacks, for even under the shadow of our boasted seats of learning at Charlottesville and Lexington, the whites of the neighboring mountains are noted for their ignorance, indigence and degradation, and the same conditions exist in the mountain regions extending from Virginia to the plains of Georgia.

If, then, we may fairly attribute our lack of prosperity to the ignorance and degradation of our laboring population, does it not naturally and inevitably follow that our poverty will continue as long as the ignorance continues, and does it not equally follow that our expectation of prosperity will be a delusion until we elevate this population? And does it not further follow that as cause always acts logically we cannot elevate unless we take the logical and necessary steps leading to that end? Nature demands an equivalent always, and in enforcing her requirements she understands what Shylock, sharp Jew as he was, never learned — viz: how to get her pound of flesh without one drop of blood. However disagreeable, painful, and even repugnant things may be to us, they are all equally agreeable to Nature, and when Nature prescribes any medicine or course, however nauseous it may be, we must follow it or ignominiously fail. Nature requires that if we want bread we must not sow wheat in May, or if we want cotton we must not plant it in August; we may do it, but if we do Nature says: Be ye hungry and be ye naked. Nature never allows us to gather figs when we have sowed thistles, nor grapes when we have planted thorns; nor, on the other hand, does she compel us to a diet of thorns and thistles when we have diligently set out orchards and planted vineyards.

Thus our prosperity is bound up in the elevation of our laboring population; and we desire prosperity. Nature says to us, You are welcome to prosperity, just as much so as if you lived in New York, Massachusetts, or Ohio; but you must pay the price thereof just as these states have done, and just as every other community must do. There are no deadheads with me. The South replies: Yes, we want prosperity, but we want it by letting our laboring population remain pretty much as they are. Nature responds: No, that won't answer; you are not even paying a penny for an immense good; you must pay the full price, which is the elevation of the people who do your work. We can't dodge the question, and we can't fool nature. We must follow her full prescription. We may, indeed, throw the medicine into the bucket, but if we do we still remain invalids.

Now as we go along we will endeavor to point out clearly what must be done to elevate our laboring population. Some of the steps we have already taken — some in full, some only partially — but we are still proceeding in the right way. Other steps we will take after reflection and a little time given; other steps, again, will require a pretty strong effort, but they, too, will be taken; but some we — that is, the older generations — will positively refuse to take, and will vehemently swear not only that we cannot, but by the Eternal, as Old Hickory used to say, we will not take them.

As we go along we will point out the various steps thought necessary, and we hope that careful attention will be given, and that we may candidly weigh all that is said, for if we do not we might in our willfulness overlook, or, because they are nauseous, deliberately refuse to take one or more essential steps, and thus render vain all our other efforts. If what is said be not of truth and wisdom, it will come to naught, and the writer will be the only sufferer, or, in the language of a higher authority: "For if this counsel or this work be of men, it will come to naught, but if it be of God, ye cannot overthrow it." [1]

[1] The Acts of the Apostles, 5:38-39.

CHAPTER VII

Can the Negro be Elevated? — Examples of Progress Here — Field Slaves Improvement on Relatives in Africa — House Slaves an Improvement on Field Slaves, and Freedmen Great Improvement on House Slaves — Examples of Progress in Africa — Causes of Negro Degradation and of White Elevation — Status of the Negro in Europe and Brazil — Full Equality — Example of Society in Rio — Progress not Inalienable to Whites.

In treating of the elevation of our laboring population, I shall confine myself to the elevation of the Negro, for though the elevation of our illiterate whites is also essential for our full prosperity, yet their elevation, as a matter of course, in a measure precedes that of the blacks. The simple willingness of the whites to elevate the Negro at once places them on a higher plane, and is a great step in advance for them, and as the additional necessary measures for the elevation of the Negro are carried out, so their own elevation, proceeding from an enlightened and liberalized public sentiment, will also progress at a rapid rate.

It is a highly favorable augury of a bright future that, owing to a liberalized sentiment, the lot of the Negro has in some parts of the South, notably in Virginia, been greatly improved. A vast interval separates the Negro of today from the Negro of twenty years ago, and as the state has suffered no detriment from his elevation so far, it should be an encouragement for all good citizens to take the other necessary steps to bridge over the still vast chasm between what he now is, and what he must be, before he can become an enlightened and full-developed citizen; before he can become that efficient producer of wealth which is absolutely essential for our own prosperity.

But before treating of the elevation of the Negro, let us first consider whether he is capable of elevation, for there is a widespread public sentiment that he is capable of only a very moderate improvement — that as we have known him, so he must ever be; and if this opinion be true, then we had better at once shut up all his schools, and at once cease all efforts for his amelioration, for they must necessarily prove fruitless.

We will not, however, indulge in theory or quote stock sacred texts, showing the equality of all men, and therefore the equality of the Negro, or quote the assertion of evolutionists that all men have sprung from one human pair, but we will appeal to a few simple facts patent to all.

First, no one will deny that even our field hands were greatly superior to their relatives in Africa, and why? Simply because our Negroes had for many years been comfortably fed and clad, and the slaves had learned something from their white masters.

Second, no one will deny that house servants, especially those raised in the family, were greatly superior in appearance and every other respect to field hands, and why? Simply because their comforts had been much greater, and their associations had been more intimate with the better class of whites.

And third, when on Sundays, we enter Negro churches and behold large, well-dressed, and well-behaved congregations presided over by pastors of good standing and ability; when we observe their numerous benevolent societies successfully conducted; when we enter their schools and see large numbers of obedient pupils, diligently studying their books, and when in their high schools we see exhibitions of scholarship creditable to the whites, with all their present and antecedent advantages, we must confess that here is an immense advance upon the house servant class. But although the interval between these last and the naked savages ranging African jungles and starving or subsisting mainly upon vermin is as great as from pole to pole, yet they are the same Negroes which many of us claim are incapable of elevation, and all the difference between these antipodes is that our Negroes have been exposed to many fostering surroundings. Now, nobody can deny that here is some elevation or improvement of our Negroes, whether we call it ten, twenty or fifty per cent, and granting that the Negro has advanced only ten per cent under slightly favoring influences, who can deny the probability, nay, the certainty, of his advancing the whole scale of one hundred per cent if exposed to the same favoring influences the whites have enjoyed for centuries; and as only good can come to the whites from the Negro's elevation, we should honestly and even zealously take all the steps necessary to that end? The proposition that twice two is four is very simple; but if we admit, also, that twice four is eight *because* twice two is four, we have a very small key, yet one that is sufficient for unlocking the most secret chambers of nature, and of explaining all the laws of the universe; so if we admit the simple proposition that our Negroes have been elevated even slightly above their brethren now dwelling in Africa, we furnish the believers in the complete elevation of the Negro with a key that may, and that probably will, unloose all the formidable bars and bolts that at present obstruct his elevation.

But those who claim that the Negro is incapable of material elevation point triumphantly to the fact that in the long course of history the Negro has accomplished nothing in the line of civilization, and they argue that if in the long past he has developed very slightly, if at all, therefore he will accomplish as little, which is nothing, in the long future.

While granting, but with some reservations, however, the general fact of the Negro's small advance, the THEREFORE, or the deduction, is demurred to, on the ground that it is a *non sequitur*. If the Negro has shown NO capacity for development from the lowest stage in which any of the family is found, then the *therefore* is logical and indisputable; but if the Negro has shown anywhere *any* development from his lowest stage of bestiality, then the *therefore* is not only illogical, but the simple fact of any improvement is an incontrovertible argument for further improvement; and the further improvement is an incontrovertible argument for further and still further improvement, until at last equality with the highest type of mankind is reached.

Let us inquire briefly into the facts. Does every tribe or people in its native home, Africa, exhibit one dead level of immovable and unredeemable barbarism? If they do, the question of the elevation of the Negro is settled at the outset; but if they do not, the game is just begun. That they do not, but that some Negroes show considerable advance, is proved from the following extract from Herbert Spencer, in his chapter on "Idol Worship and Fetich Worship":

We find it (Fetichism) rampant when there are fortified towns, well-organized governments, large standing armies, prisons, police and sumptuary laws, considerable division of labor, periodical markets, regular shops and all the appliances, showing some progress in civilization.[1]

Also by same in "Political Institutions" (Chapter I):

Take, again, an African society — Dahomey. We find there a finished system of classes, six in number; complex governmental arrangements, with officials always in pairs; an army divided into battalions, having reviews and sham fights; prisons, police and sumptuary laws; an agriculture which uses manure and grows a score kind of plants; moated towns, bridges and roads with turnpikes.[2]

Again, in Chapter II, quoting Baker:

[1] Herbert Spencer, *The Principles of Sociology* (Third Ed.), I-1, p. 323, in *Synthetic Philosophy* (Westminster Ed., New York and London, n.d.) (Ed.)
[2] *Ibid.*, II-1, p. 237. (Ed.)

Passing suddenly from the wildest savagedom to semi-civilization, we come to Unyoro, where they have developed administration sub-governors, taxes, good clothing, art, agriculture, architecture.[3]

Besides these, there are the Abyssinians, the Ashantees, and the Zulus — all peoples who have defied the power of Great Britain, and who have developed into strong and stable, though bloody and despotic, governments. If circumstances in Africa itself have elevated some Negro tribes into powerful kingdoms, the argument, instead of being that the Negro is incapable of improvement, is that he is capable of elevation, and that this elevation is proportioned to and dependent upon favorable surroundings, acting continuously for long periods of time.

But lest the reader be wearied, let us conclude this point with a most inadequate summary in parallel columns of the surroundings of whites and blacks, and then let us wonder, if we can, that the two colors are now as we find them, and then question that if the surroundings had been reversed whether we would not now be found at the bottom and the blacks at the top of civilization.

NATURAL SURROUNDINGS

WHITES	BLACKS
Temperate zone.	Torrid zone.
Stimulating climate.	Debilitating climate.
Man invigorated by climate; therefore,	Man overpowered and degraded by climate; therefore,

[3] *Ibid.*, p. 249. Blair omits several phrases in this sentence without indicating the omission but without changing the meaning essentially. (ED.)

Bold, free, energetic, intelligent.	Timid, slavish, indolent, stupid.
Many navigable streams.	No navigable streams.
Coasts deeply indented with gulfs, bays, sounds, and, therefore,	One unbroken coastline, no bays, gulfs, sounds, and, therefore,
People encouraged to industry and accumulating wealth.	People sluggish and slothful, no encouragement to labor and no accumulation of wealth.

ARTIFICIAL SURROUNDINGS

Freedom of person.	Abject slavery of person.
Laboring for self.	Toiling for others.
Hope of reward and prospect of advancement.	Little hope of reward and no prospect of advancement.
Wealth, with its innumerable advantages.	Indigence, with its numberless drawbacks.
Fostering influences of every kind.	Debasing influences of every kind.
Weight of society light.	Weight of society crushing.

The Caucasian, but especially that branch of the family which dwells in the United States, like the Egyptians, Assyrians, Persians, Greeks and Romans of the old world, and like the Chinese of both the ancient and modern world (for the Chinese whom we think unworthy to breathe the free air of heaven in our glorious country appear to have been a powerful empire long before the first stone of the pyramid of Cheops was laid, long before Helen was ravished from ante-classic Greece, and long before Lupa, untrue to her nature, nursed instead of devoured Romulus and Remus), fondly but falsely imagines that his race is the favored child of heaven, and that the Almighty himself has especially, particularly, and exclusively endowed it with all the powers and capacities of civilization. But the real fact is, our remote ancestors were as scurvy a lot as ever scourged the earth, and even our medieval ancestors were a roving set of pirates and freebooters, whose lives were spent in ravishing and then murdering women, in slaying infants and old men, and in reducing to slavery all able-bodied men who escaped the edge of the sword; and the civilization of us, the descendants of these monsters, is solely owing to favoring and fostering influences, mainly those of commerce, operating through centuries of time.

We laugh at the Chinese for the vanity of claiming celestial origin for their kingdom and emperor, but our vanity is much greater. The Chinese draw the line at King and State, but we, more civilized, but less modest, draw the line of divine favor so deftly that it will embrace all whites of any and every degree, but at the same time exclude each and all of every other color.

But although nowhere in the United States, either North or South, does the Negro enjoy all the rights of the white, yet when we cast our eyes beyond the limits of our country, the supposed home of the free, we find the Negro occupying the status of *full* equality. In England and in France, countries which have led in the race of civilization and of liberty, and which are still in the van of enlightenment, the Negro rests under no political or social ban, but is received everywhere according to his merits and credentials, and if the Negro has good letters of introduction he will be received everywhere, while the white man, if not so provided, will be totally ignored. And in the empire of Brazil, whose ruler has a world-wide reputation for goodness and wisdom, the Negro is accorded full social and political equality. A Virginian, who was for eight years from 1853 United States consul at Rio, tells me that when he was there one of the emperor's ministers and one of the court physicians were black Negroes; that he had danced with Negroes at parties and official receptions, and that many of them, educated in Europe and favored with wealth, were much more elegantly cultured than he was himself.

And let not such who disbelieve the capacity of the Negro for elevation imagine that perpetual progress is the inalienable inheritance of the Caucasian, who as implicitly believes that he is the favored child of heaven as do the almond-eyed Celestials, for the slightest acquaintance with history and with the career of individuals around them must convince them that a people grows in wealth and power as long as favoring influences predominate, and declines when adverse influences prevail. Greece, in her days of imperishable renown, and Greece in her abject humiliation under Turkish rule, is one of many striking illustrations of this truth as applied to nations, and we almost daily have equally striking illustrations as regards the individual when we see the individual and the family falling through poverty, vice or recklessness from the top to the bottom of society.

If there is any truth in experience, then experience teaches that the Negro, degraded as we think him, and degraded as he really is, can be elevated when exposed to the same fostering influences that have surrounded us.

CHAPTER VIII

Why not let Time Elevate? — Our Lives too Short — Must Hasten and Assist Natural Process of Time — Elevation cannot be Summary; must have Cordial Co-operation of the Whites — Elevation of the Negro does not mean Negro Domination — Why?

Seeing now that the Negro can be elevated — seeing that he has been elevated, elevation and degradation being simply the logical consequences of favorable or adverse agencies — what are we going to do? Shall we oppose or shall we drift and take chances of killing or curing, or shall we promote the Negro's progress? Prejudice counsels the first, timidity the second, common sense the third; so what shall we do?

The majority will probably say, Wait; why take any steps to correct any abuses or to counteract any injurious consequences associated with his present degraded condition, for (say they) evils will in time cure themselves. But although history and observation abundantly prove that evils do not always work their own cure, but as often or oftener effect the ruin of the patient, we will admit that time will happily effect a solution of the Negro problem; but then we must remember that time is not only a very uncertain, but also a very long, something, and while we are waiting for this time we will be really suffering all the evils and disadvantages of actual poverty, which should not be thought of. In all other things we endeavor to abridge the natural process of time, and so should we in the gravest question before us — namely, the elevation of the Negro.

If our lives lengthened into centuries, like those of the patriarchs, there might be little cause for haste, for one generation would have ample time to witness the perfection of this and of many other reforms; but when, in these degenerate days, man's span is shortened to a paltry three score years and ten, a generation, if things are left to drift, will pass away before it can see one single reform of importance accomplished. Thus, if we take no steps to hasten the Negro's perfect enfranchisement and elevation, upon which our power and prosperity are dependent, not only this but most probably other generations will disappear before we will escape from our present condition of poverty and ignorance, already partially set forth. Man's life is now too short to wait for the natural process of time, which may or may not work a cure, but he must hasten nature and take a hand himself, and he does, when wise, take a hand, and greatly to his advantage. If the elevation of the Negro would not make us wealthy and prosperous, instead of advocating his cause it would be the part of wisdom to promote any and all measures that would tend speedily to wipe him off the face of the earth; for to remain as he is, is not to be a citizen, but, in spite of the ballot, to be a serf; and to remain as he is, is to be a clog upon the South in her efforts to become wealthy, powerful, and respected by the other portions of the Union, and by the world at large. At present we are contemned by more than half the United States, and are totally ignored by the world.

The measures necessary for the elevation of the Negro cannot be carried out summarily or by simple act of legislation, but they require time, care, wisdom and patience, and are impossible without the acquiescence and cordial co-operation of the whites. The Negroes might be given the full benefit of their numbers, so that they absolutely controlled all the Southern States, either by numerical superiority or by combination with a minority of the whites, but, with the whites opposed, they could not hold power for any length of time, for the superior intellect and stronger will of the whites would soon, through intimidation or fraud, or by both, cow and scatter their leaders, when the Negroes, being like sheep without shepherds, would, if the contest had been long and embittered, be in danger of actual bondage. Great as is the power of the National Government, it cannot elevate the Negroes itself, nor can it force the whites to do so. The question is, we may say, absolutely within control of the whites. They can keep the Negro in his present degraded condition, but they cannot do so without at the same time laying the axe at the root of their own welfare; and they can crush, but while doing this, they will be like Samson, who could destroy his enemies only by destroying himself.

The whites cannot see this now, for they are dominated by a great apprehension — namely, that the elevation of the Negro means the degradation of the whites — and until this fear is allayed by showing them that little probable harm can accrue to them thereby, it will be like appealing to the winds to urge them to steps leading to the complete elevation and enfranchisement of the Negro. In spite of all exhortation to love our neighbor as ourself, human nature will persist in loving itself better than its neighbor, and so, as long as the Southern people believe that the complete elevation of the Negro will be an injury to them, they cannot be expected to take kindly, or even to take at all, to the idea. Show one that his interest lies in a certain direction, and there is little difficulty in getting him to go that way. Even religion is in vain unless it can show the sinner that it will confer an actual benefit upon him either here or elsewhere; and so to elevate the Negro, we must show the whites that his elevation will be no detriment to them, and to prove this is the whole tenor and object of this essay.

There is, however, one error, or rather delusion, that we must guard against. To elevate the Negro will, of course, greatly lessen the interval between the two colors; but because the gap will thereby be diminished, we must not jump at the illogical conclusion that the gap will be lessened by the debasement in any manner of the whites. We unconsciously, but logically, reason to ourselves that to elevate partially necessarily means to elevate completely; that if we raise the Negro even so little as ten per cent there is no logical stopping point short of one hundred per cent; that, therefore, in time the two races will most probably meet on the same plane; but we must not infer, for that would be an error, that this plane will be reached by ascent of the Negro and descent of the white, both meeting on a common plane a little higher than midway between the two. It is difficult not so to conclude, because it is instinctive with us, but though instinct may and does answer for brutes, it is a very poor guide for human beings. There never was a greater delusion than this instinctive apprehension of deterioration of the whites; for bad as human nature is, it does not voluntarily desert the higher and the better for the lower and the worse. As a localism here has it: You can't fool one with corn bread when biscuits are on the table. The colors will not meet halfway or anywhere near it, but the smaller and weaker will gravitate to the bigger and stronger, just as in the material world, and in time the Negro will probably rise to the plane of the white. Blind and selfish human nature, which is honey-combed with envy and jealousy, will object to seeing the Negro anything better than a despised and de-graded creature, speaking with bated breath and bow-ing with head uncovered at its slightest nod, and such nature, already degraded, will, of course, feel itself humiliated when it loses its arbitrary hold upon its former dependents, but enlightened human nature will not be and will not feel itself degraded because the Negro has been enabled through merit to climb up to the higher plane, any more than a gentleman will feel degraded because his carpenter, butcher, shoe-maker, or whatnot, builds a handsome home next door; on the contrary, a gentleman will rejoice that such a social inferior had by intelligence and industry elevated himself in the social scale.

CHAPTER IX

To Elevate must Inspire with Hope and Self-Respect — Negro has Little of Either — Caste — The South a Land of Caste and Privilege — All Whites in Highest, all Negroes in Lowest Caste.

Before we can make men of depraved and degraded human beings, be they Negro, Semite, or even Caucasian, and therefore efficient producers of wealth, there are three principal things to be done. They must be inspired with self-respect, their hope must be stimulated and their intelligence must be cultivated, and especially so with the Negro, for his self-respect is feeble, his hope faint, and his intelligence slight; he must economically, morally, and socially be born again, and self-respect, hope and intelligence are the trinity that will work out his elevation, and they are also the rule of three to work out our own material regeneration.

Self-respect is, in general terms, that quality that prevents our stealing, lying, drunkenness, idling, neglecting family, etc., and the man that is materially lacking in self-respect is generally little better than rotten driftwood, and incapable of accomplishing any good for the society in which he lives. In passing, we mention that two of our greatest men have been singular and contradictory examples of this influence of self-respect. Washington possessed it to such an abnormal degree he was almost unapproachable, and Jupiter himself, in his severest moods, was addressed by his inferior deities with scarce more reverence than was Washington by his associates. On the other hand, General Grant at one period of his early military life was so lacking in self-respect that his fellow-officers obliged him to place his resignation in their hands to be held *in terrorem* over him, and yet they were finally obliged to forward it to headquarters. His subsequent career for many years was a painful exhibition of the effects of the lack of self-respect.

Hope is, in general terms, that sentiment that leads us to expect rewards from our exertions, and that stimulates us to effort. When hope is faint we can accomplish little, and when hope is extinct we slavishly submit to fate and sheepishly yield all that we have, even our lives, to the first comer. But where hope is strong, and where we can reasonably expect an adequate return for our labor, there we witness abounding prosperity, as in the commercial and manufacturing sections of our country, and indeed in all new countries; and where hope, even though dead, revives, we behold the same Grant emerge from poverty and degradation and become the greatest soldier of recent times.

Intelligence is, in general terms, that fruit of the training of the nervous system, of which the brain is merely the crown, which enables us to perceive objects and situations in their true light and relationship; which enables us to grasp and avail ourselves of attending circumstances that will assist us to accomplish our object with the least expenditure, and which enables us to perceive and to avoid those difficulties and impediments that will thwart us altogether, or that will cause us to expend unnecessary effort.

The Negro is greatly deficient in all these cardinal qualifications. His self-respect is so small he pays little regard to chastity or the marriage vow, and bastardy is very general; he pays little regard to honesty, and when his necessities or his inclinations combine with opportunity, the difference between *meum et tuum* is reduced to its least expression; and he pays little regard for truth, for he looks upon lying and deceit as very venial faults, if indeed they be faults at all.

And what hope has the Negro, and what stimulus does it exert upon him? Alas, in the present attitude of public sentiment he can have but little hope, and hope can supply him with small incentive. And why? Because he is looked upon with contempt as a degraded inferior simply by virtue of having a black skin. A Negro may be learned, pious or distinguished; he may have rendered great services to his country or to humanity; he may be honored in England, France and Germany; but when he comes among us who are so superior to the flower of Europe, he is at once sent to Coventry. If he should obtain accommodation at hotels he receives it surreptitiously, and if any family, be it clerical, professional or mercantile, should receive him except as an inferior and as an act of condescension, as we sometimes invite inferiors to take a seat in our presence, that family is at once, or would be, put under the social ban. Not only if one is a Negro, but if he has, or is even suspected to have, one drop of Negro blood, he is placed under almost every disadvantage, and he can never feel safe from snubs, insults, or even kicks from the superior whites. In other words, the Negro is the victim of caste.

In countries where caste prevails, there is little hope of progress for the inferior castes, and none at all for the lowest caste of all. In such countries, if people are born in a stable, they and their descendants are doomed to remain forever in a stable, and if they happen to be born in a higher station, there they remain perpetually. In India, *the* land of castes, the Brahmin is the highest caste; and whether rich or poor, whether a menial or a lordly idler, neither he nor his neighbors ever forget the fact; and such is the power, such is the influence, of caste that though he be cook to the viceroy from far distant Albion, he regards himself and is considered by his fellows as superior even to the august and powerful Governor-General, who in great measure controls the destinies of his millions of feeble and helpless brethren (252,541,210, census 1881).

The South, also, is a veritable land of caste, and its chains hang heavily upon those of the lowest caste. In the palmy days of slavery, when one man held in his hand the lives of a thousand, there were several castes; but now, though there are still many social and other gradations, there are primarily only two castes.

Then there was first in rank and influence the caste of educated and wealthy planters, who assumed the airs and imitated the manners of the most exclusive aristocracy of England and France, whence their families had immigrated. In Virginia, Louisiana and South Carolina, but especially in the last state, many were highly cultivated and intellectual, were polished and refined to a high degree, the men being elegant and chivalric, and the women charming and beautiful. In them we beheld all that was noble and attractive in the system of caste. Next came an intermediate caste of planters. They were frequently men of wealth, but without education and of little refinement, and though they met the first caste on nearly equal but yet deferential terms on the hustings and court green, the families of the two castes never thought of visiting socially. Then came the overseer caste. This caste, usually hard and heartless, was composed mainly of men who had been overseers, but who had acquired a few slaves, and had set up for themselves. Although the men mingled on semi-equal terms with those next above them, they were generally looked down upon, if not despised; and their families, as a rule, never thought of visiting socially the families of those above them. Finally came the "poor white" caste, possessed of no Negroes, but of a few acres, and despised alike by whites and blacks.

The Negroes, of course, were lower still, but they were hardly considered as human beings. They were regarded pretty much like horses and cattle, simply as instruments like them, to enable the other castes to live, some in elegance, some in ease, but all in comfort without thought and without toil. They were treated, too, pretty much as cattle; many, when the masters were kind, treated mildly and their physical necessities carefully provided for; and many, when the masters were harsh and brutal, treated with cruelty and sometimes worked or beaten to death, it being a maxim with some cotton planters that it was cheaper to work a Negro to death and buy another than to work him reasonably and prolong his life.

But now, in the new order of things, all these castes have become amalgamated into one, and a new caste has been formed of those who were formerly considered too low to form a caste at all, and Southern society is now virtually divided into two castes. In the first caste are merged indiscriminately gentleman, farmer, overseer, poor white, and each and every one of these, regardless of education, worth, refinement, decency or morality, belongs to this class simply by reason of a white skin. The second caste is composed promiscuously of all who have a black skin and all related to them, however remotely; and all who are thus marked, however cultured and refined they may be, however able and however excellent, are confined as by fate to this caste, and are not permitted to throw off its galling chains; and society, by its inexorable verdict, decrees that the meanest, lowest, and most degraded of the first caste are, *ipso facto*, the irreversible and perpetual superiors of the best, highest and ablest of the second caste.

Hope cannot exist, certainly cannot flourish, under such a weight. If he is to remain forever a "nigger," an object of undisguised contempt, even to the lowest whites, the Negro will naturally say to himself, Why strive, why labor, why practice painful self-denial in order to rise, if I am to derive no good from my effort? On the contrary, he will not exert himself, but will sink into despondency, and instead of becoming a net producer, and thus an instrument of our own prosperity, he will continue as he is, a depredator upon others' industry and a consumer of wealth. The

South can never become prosperous, with its laboring population bereft of hope. Without hope the proudest Anglo-Saxon sinks into despair — much more the helpless Negro, who is little more than a child.

CHAPTER X

If Highest Caste will not Elevate, must Crush Lowest Caste to Powder — Race Prejudice must be Mollified and Obliterated — Prejudice Mark of Inferiority — Courts of Justice must be Impartial to All Colors — Why Negroes do not Enjoy such Impartiality — Whites Kind to Negroes Individually, but Kindness must be Accepted as Inferiors.

If the Negro is not to be elevated to the full standard, then clap on the shackles again and reduce him speedily to bondage when he can be made to work; no, not reduce him to slavery, because all history proves that slavery is finally destructive of the master caste, but put him between the upper and the nether millstone, turn on the water, and quickly grind him out of existence, for otherwise he must necessarily become a thorn in the side of society; for having once tasted the sweets of partial enfranchisement, he will not cease his efforts to obtain complete enfranchisement and equality until they are crowned with success, or until he is again reduced to abject submission. This period of trial or probation may continue for a few years, or it may be indefinitely, but whether it lasts for centuries or merely for years, it must be a period of anxiety and impoverishment for the whites. But the South *must* do something; it can't say, I won't do anything, or, I will fold my hands and see what will happen. The South, impelled by the current of events, has done a great deal, and it is still doing much, but a vast deal yet remains to be done, and the point is to prove to the South that it is in its interest to do this great deal more, and to do it without unnecessary delay.

The first, the most important and the most difficult step to take is to mollify and finally to obliterate race and color prejudice, a prejudice by no means peculiar to the South or to white and black races, for until very recent years the Frenchman had neither charity nor justice for the Englishman, though separated only by a narrow strip of water, and the Englishman reciprocated in kind and with usurious interest; and although divided by only an imaginary line, the prejudices between Englishman and Scotchman were notorious; and even today the Englishman is ruled by prejudice when Ireland and her claims are in question. But these race prejudices have now measurably disappeared, and they will finally become practically extinct as intercourse, commercial and otherwise, makes nations mutually acquainted. And not only national but personal prejudices of all kinds also disappear as intelligence is disseminated. Prejudice against color itself has quite disappeared among Latin nations, and is quite unknown in Great Britain, our worthy exemplar in so many respects, where a Negro stands on his merits like other people.

But a general exclamation will arise that prejudice against color is ineradicable, and that we can never, never overcome it. Such a confession involves two contradictory assertions, both of which are equally erroneous. It implies that we are superior to the great European nations, and in the same breath that we are inferior to them — superior in that we are too wise to follow their example and divest ourselves of prejudice against color, and inferior in that we are unwilling or unable to do so. Neither is true; and if European nations have found it wise to break down the prejudice against color it will not be wise, but foolish, for us not to follow their example; and if they have been able and willing to throw off the shackles of prejudice, we are dishonoring ourselves to say or to think that we cannot do so likewise. Many glory in prejudice, foolishly thinking it a mark of superiority, but prejudice is always a weakness, and when it is extreme it is a badge of dishonor. The prejudiced are as they are because they do not see things in their true light, and are like a horse that shies and throws its rider to death because it sees in the simple clod, stone or stump a frightful specter about to spring upon and devour it. The clearer one sees and the more enlightened he is, the freer he is from prejudice, which may be termed seeing things in a false light. And for so many generations past we have been looking upon the Negro in a false light that we cannot see him and his rights in their true light, and we shy violently and run the risk of wrecking our whole material welfare at the ideas of elevation, equality, manhood, etc., for the Negro. Southerners cannot be true to their lofty

character if either unwilling or incapable of overcoming color prejudice, nor true to their interests
either.

And while mollifying and finally correcting our
prejudices, we must also modify our actions before
we can inspire the Negro with the self-respect and
hope that are essential to making him a good citizen
and an efficient producer of wealth. And the first
duty resting upon us in this respect is to see that in
criminal matters — that is to say, in matters of life
and liberty — the scales of justice hang more level
between whites and blacks; that the hand of justice
bears more equally upon the two colors, and that
both are punished alike for similar offenses, although
it would seem reasonable to inflict heavier penalties
upon the whites because they occupy a much higher
plane morally, socially and intellectually, and are
therefore less excusable for violating law; and we
must see that our courts of justice, the most august
and beneficent product of civilization, are an equal
refuge for the wronged of all colors, and an equal
terror to all wrong-doers, irrespective of previous
condition.

And is not the law the same for all; and does it
make any distinction between rich and poor, white
and black? Literally, the law is the same for all. Then
what more can be desired? The trouble is not that the
laws are partial, though some of their enactments —
namely, the whipping-post, chain-gang and poll tax
laws — were aimed principally against the Negro; but
the trouble is with the interpretation of the laws by
the juries, who merely voice public sentiment, which
is superior to the law itself. The average jury is a

whimsical creature, subject to all kinds of influences, though mostly of a sentimental character. In criminal matters where whites are concerned, it seems ever to lean to the defense; and the strongest arguments of the prosecution are easily offset and upset by appeals on behalf of youth, family, station, respectability, etc.; or perhaps the whole family, weeping, is placed in full view of the jury; and the susceptible jury — sure at least in such cases to weep with them that weep — speedily brings in a verdict of acquittal where guilt is clearly manifest; or it says jail where it ought to say penitentiary; or one year where it ought to say ten, and ten years where it ought to pronounce death. But the Negro has none of these sentimental advantages. Too poor to employ competent counsel, his liberty and life are necessarily committed to incompetent hands, when the proverb of "Poor pay — poor preach" becomes reality. But more unfortunate still, what sentiment can a poor, ignorant, unkempt Negro inspire? Who thinks of his family, of his wife bowed down with grief, of his little ones deprived of a father's support and suffering for bread? The idea is preposterous, and so the jury, without difficulty, brings in its verdict of jail, penitentiary, or even death. The Negro may be rightly punished, and he may receive no more than his just deserts, but if this is so, then the white receives less than his due deserts; or if the white is judged none too leniently, then the Negro is judged altogether too harshly.

As long as the Negro sees this state of affairs continue; as long as justice appears to him to slip aside her bandage when he is brought before her august tribunal, and judge him according to his previous and present condition, he must be bowed down with dread and humiliation, and whatever hope he may have nourished must die within him. But when he sees that similar offenses meet with equal punishments, irrespective of color or previous condition, then however severely he may be chastised, his self-respect and hope will not be offended; but on the contrary, they will spring up and strengthen, and make him a man — make him an efficient agent in promoting that prosperity of which we are ever dreaming but never behold. In civil suits, where the judges, in Virginia at least, practically, through their instructions, decide the case, the Negro receives substantial justice.

But are Negroes treated unfairly by juries and public opinion? Yes, and the experience and observation of every fair-minded man will confirm the assertion. One cardinal proof is that a white man seldom receives punishment for assault, however brutal, however unprovoked, however cowardly — be it maiming, homicide or murder upon a Negro — unless, forsooth, the assailant be some degraded creature, disowned by his own caste. Of the numberless instances — running into the thousands during the past twenty-three years — of homicides and murder of blacks by whites, there is no single instance of capital punishment, and few, very few, instances of imprisonment beyond a few months in jail, or a slight fine. The fact is the juries, which are the sole judges of the evidence, will accept testimony against a Negro that they would reject in the case of whites; and on the other hand they will frequently reject, or at least discredit, testimony of the Negro against the white man, however well supported it may be. But to com-

pound for sins we are inclined to by damning those
we have no mind to, in case of any difficulty between
white and black, and the former is injured or loses
his life; lucky is the latter if the homicide is not
declared by the crowd to be murder — when courts
of justice, though sure to inflict the highest penalty
in his case, are found to be too slow, and he is
dragged forth and slain, unshrived and unshriven, as
if he were a monstrous wild beast of whose presence
earth could not be rid too quickly.

As bearing on this point, the following is copied
from the Richmond *Dispatch* as I am writing this
chapter. Many other examples could be selected in
the course of another month. All these wretches
were Negroes, whom justice, entirely untempered by
mercy, would not have suffered to escape, and there
was therefore absolutely no excuse and no necessity
for these assassinations:

[Special telegram to the Dispatch.]

RALEIGH, N. C., September 14 — News was received here tonight of another lynching, which is the
thirteenth this year. It occurred at Whiteville, Columbus
county, night before last. A body of masked men, a hundred or more, entered the jail and demanded the keys
from the jailer. With a score of revolvers pointed at him
he surrendered the keys, and the lynchers went to the cell
where Sherman Farrier (colored) was confined for an
outrage committed on an aged white woman, took him
and departed. Yesterday, suspended to the limb of a large
oak about one mile from the jail, the body of Sherman
Farrier was found with a placard pinned on his breast
bearing the words: "We protect the virtue of our women.
Beware." Farrier was a man of bad character, and had

repeatedly been engaged in robbery. He was given a pre-liminary hearing before two magistrates last Monday, and was committed to jail to await trial. The evidence against him was conclusive.

We will here mention a singular phase of Southern white life, and that is, the slain or injured is *always* the guilty party, and nowhere else in the wide world does justice so accurately apportion penalty. The slain *must* be the guilty party, for the white slayer of his white brother is never punished, or hardly ever, and is almost always acquitted with honor. Acquittal usually means innocence, but universal acquittal can only mean universal innocence, and universal guilt of the maimed or slain. As a matter of fact, it is safer in the South for a respectable white man to slay his neighbor than to kill his neighbor's dog; for killing the man rarely means more than a short time in jail, a feeble trial, and an acquittal with *éclat*, of course a round legal fee; but killing the dog means almost as generally an accounting with the owner of the dog, in which case the murderous revolver may take an active part.

But let it not be supposed from the foregoing that the whites individually are not just to the Negro; they are much more considerate of his wants and feelings than are Northern people. But as a rule our kindness is bestowed as condescension, and it must be received with all due humility and with a tacit ac-knowledgment of inferiority of status; for let the Negro betray even a moderate sense of equality or manhood, he is then thought "impudent," and our kindness takes affront. Until the Negro sees and feels that the community fully recognizes that courts of justice are as much a refuge for him and as much a bulwark of his life and liberty as for the highest and the proudest, he can never feel sure of his position; and as long as what he enjoys is by favor or condescension, he can never be certain that what he enjoys today may not be arbitrarily wrested from him tomorrow; and not until he sees that what he enjoys is by inalienable right can he have that sense of security and manhood that is essential for an efficient wealth-producer.

CHAPTER XI

Other Things we must Do — The Negroes should be Allowed Free Admission to All Hotels, Theatres, Churches, and Official Receptions — Such Places not Private Property — Why they Belong to the Whole Public — Why Negroes should not be restricted to Places for Negroes — If so, Same Principle of Segregation should be Applied to Other Things and to People of Each State — Example of Drummer — Imaginary Examples, etc.

The Negro must be allowed free access to all hotels and other places of public entertainment; he must be allowed free admittance to all theatres and other places of public amusement; he must be allowed free entrance to all churches, and in all public and official receptions of president, governor, mayor, etc., he must not be excluded by a hostile caste sentiment. In all these things and in all these places he must, unless we wish to clip his hope and crush his self-respect, be treated precisely like the whites, no better, but no worse.

In the capital of our great country, the respectable Negro, though not welcomed, is admitted to the best hotels, to the best seats in theatres, to the best churches, and in presidential receptions he meets with no humiliating discriminations; yet when we come South as far as Richmond, only about 100 miles from Washington, we seem to be in a different country, we seem to be translated from a world of equality where worth makes the man to a land of caste where birth makes him. In Richmond a riot is threatened when it is thought that a Negro member of a Brooklyn white lodge intends occupying, in company with his white brother, a first-class seat in the theatre. The hotels, except under extraordinary pressure, drive Negroes from their doors; the leading congregations, except the Catholic, would go into a spasm and perhaps leave the house, were the Negro to seat himself with the body of meek and lowly worshipers; and if a Negro with his wife or sweetheart were to attend the governor's public reception, they would in a few minutes be the only guests, or they would be frozen, if not driven, out. But perhaps we should not be surprised that such slight change of latitude should work such great difference, seeing that a slight variation at the creation produced all the vast difference between man and woman.

Let us put ourselves in the Negro's place. Let us feel when passing good hotels there is no admission here; we dare not go in lest we be kicked out; when entering a theatre to be told to go up in the top gallery, no seat for you in the parquette; when entering an imposing church to be told rudely no place in God's house for you, unless there be a gallery, to which you are sent with indifference; or when seeking to attend an official reception, *your* governor's for instance, to be told brusquely no admittance; and suppose this treatment is continued year after year, and as far as we can see is likely to continue *ad infinitum*, would not we have our pride cut to the quick, and would not our morale be greatly lowered, and would we not be greatly handicapped in all our efforts to get along? There can be no doubt of it; and can we expect the ignorant, degraded, poverty-ridden Negro to rise with such burdens resting upon him, and if he sees no prospect of the burdens' lifting? Hope herself will not be able to stimulate him to exertion. We must lift these burdens, heavy and grievous to be borne, and unless we do we can never have the Negroes as co-workers in the production of wealth, and without their co-operation it will be vain to expect prosperity. We may continue to crush, and we may delight in the exhibition of our arbitrary power, but every oppression and every denial of the equal rights of the Negroes will be at our own expense.

Many will excuse and defend this treatment of the Negro on the ground that theatres, hotels and churches are private property, and that to compel them to receive Negroes on equal terms with whites would be to correct one wrong, if it be a wrong to treat them thus, by committing another. But although theatres, hotels and churches may be private property, they are public as regards their creation and their functions, and they are of the nature of railways, which may be private property, but which are public institutions. As a railroad cannot build a track or run a car except by virtue of permission, called a charter, granted by the public, so no theatre can raise its curtain and no hotel can spread its table without the same permission, called a license, from the public, which means not some, but all the people, not whites alone, but whites and blacks. And churches are likewise public, because the community, which means all the people, exempts them from all taxation, and churches can become strictly private only by renouncing their public exemptions, and then they may impose any restrictions they choose upon would-be worshipers.

All these institutions are public — they belong to the public, and are for the public convenience — and they can as properly refuse accommodation to all whose noses indicate a Semitic origin, all whose names or "rich brogue" betray Hibernian descent, or all whose "sweet accent" à la General Scott[1] reveals Teutonic birth, as to refuse similar accommodation to all whose faces are black.

For public sentiment to shut the doors of any of these places in the faces of any portion of the community is to degrade and to humiliate it, and is greatly to impair its ability to serve the best interests of society. But granting these institutions to be private property, their owners would not be injured when all were obliged to furnish similar accommodations to all classes, for in that case, caste purists would then have no occasion to desert one place for another, for they would be liable to meet everywhere the despised black face. Would I like being thrown with Negroes at the same hotels and other places? No, but it would be very much easier to bear the shock to taste or fancy than to endure the shock to justice by depriving any fellow-creatures of their rights.

But others say let the Negroes stick to their own

[1] I can only speculate that this is a misprint for "Schurz," General Carl Schurz, who was of German origin. (ED.)

hotels, their own places of public amusement, and their own churches. As a rule they will do so, for like prefers like the world over. But suppose some Negroes on account of convenience, comfort or profit desire to go elsewhere, what then? Shall we say no, and in case of refusal shall we call in the police, and in a place like New York herd them together in Thompson Street and other local ghettos?

This course would present a pretty state of affairs. Policemen would increase prodigiously in number, and blue cloth and brass buttons would rise to a monstrous price, for constables would be required at all the approaches to every city and town where Negroes would likely travel in order to direct them to their appropriate places. In small cities this would not be very difficult, but in New York, where distances are very great, the policemen, instead of guarding the city, would be employed in guiding the colored traveler, or, as many travelers would certainly prove refractory, would be engaged in dragging them to stationhouses, which would then be so full of prisoners whose only crime was a matter of taste, that there would be no room for actual criminals. Cities, too, would be obliged sometimes to increase their debts on account of damages for false imprisonment, for dark brunettes are so much like mulattoes, mistakes are sure to occur frequently, like the following:

Some years ago a drummer, from my city [Richmond], since become partner in his house, was urging an irascible North Carolina merchant to purchase his wares. He was, however, a little too persistent, and vexed the merchant, who cried out to him, "You damned yaller rascal, if you don't get out of here I'll

kick you out." Before adopting the plan of segregation, our dark-skinned [white] Southern brethren
should carefully reflect, for they might be corralled
and introduced to the charms of Thompson Street.

If the system of segregation were adopted for the
blacks, it would be well to extend its benefits to the
people of all this glorious Union. There are thirty-
eight states, all of whose citizens have more or less
peculiarities, some of which are very offensive to the
citizens of other states. Now, for the peace, comfort
and quiet of the citizen, great cities like New York
and Chicago should be divided into thirty-eight sections, properly marked, branded or painted — paint-
ing would be the most effective and picturesque, so
that no town need ever be painted a uniform red —
and when a train or boat arrived, the hackmen should
not cry out Astor House, Fifth Avenue Hotel, etc.,
but the travelers should sing out Georgia, Ohio, New
York, Massachusetts, etc., etc., when they would be
taken in charge by the custodians of the various sections and properly directed. Then nobody would be
shocked by color, whiskey, tobacco juice, profanity
or any other habit, practice or forms of speech they
were not accustomed to at home. Obviously, a modi-
fication of the plan would have to be made in small
places like Richmond, and in the Southern cities.
These cities cannot afford many hotels, and as visitors
cannot be segregated, Yankees, Hoosiers, Wolverines,
etc., should be refused admittance to any Southern
hotel, because in the first place, they are not fit to
associate even in hotels with high-toned Southerners;
in the second place, because their "guessing," "hadn't
ought tos," "do tells," etc., would clash painfully with

our "few molasses," "haven't saws," "we-uns," "you-uns," etc.; and because in the third place, their criticisms, verbal or by looks, of our favorite pastime of medallioning our floors with tobacco juice would be extremely disagreeable; and while excluding color because disagreeable or offensive, it would be well to exclude at the same time everything else distasteful, so that our hotel life may realize the ideal of perfect social intercourse. But what shall we do with visitors from Northern and Western states, whom the frantic efforts of our immigration societies induce to come South? That is easy enough. Partition off in the suburbs camping grounds or caravansaries for the various Northern and Western states, and tell them to bring their tents and "vittles" along. This would be a very nice arrangement, and the novelty of it would undoubtedly attract strangers from all parts of the world. Segregation is indeed an excellent plan, and the more excellent the more generally should its benefits be diffused.[2]

[2] The irony is heavy-handed in this and the previous page, but it *is* irony. (Ed.)

CHAPTER XII

Negro Votes Freely in Virginia, North Carolina, and Tennessee, but not in the Six Southern States; Why? — Tables Showing Population, Voting, State and Congressional Representation in Three Southern and Six Other Southern States — Similar Tables for New York and Massachusetts and for Ohio and Illinois — Bad Effects of Not Voting — All should be Encouraged to Vote — Examples — Ballot to Virginia Negro Stands for Everything Great, Good and Glorious — Cultivation of Tobacco makes Virginia Negro Eager to Vote — Cultivation of Cotton makes South Carolina and Georgia Negro Apathetic — Religion may make South Carolina and Georgia Negro Indifferent to Ballot — Example of what South Carolina and Georgia Negro Yields for sake of Religion — Negroes of the Six Southern States only Apostolic Christians.

There is another right the Negro does not fully enjoy in all parts of the South: this is the right preservative of all rights —

THE RIGHT OF THE BALLOT

In Virginia, North Carolina and Tennessee, the Negro, led by able and strong white minorities, exercises this right freely, and as few frauds are perpetrated to his injury as the two parties North and West practice against each other. But from South Carolina to Texas, the Negro appears to have been as completely deprived of his electoral rights as have the whites been deprived of his servile labor.[1]

The following tables would seem to prove this. The first table is of the three states where the Negro enjoys his electoral rights; the second one is of the other six Southern states east of the Mississippi, where it is believed the Negro is deprived of his vote:

Males twenty-one and upwards Census 1880		Congressional election 1886		Legislature 1887-88		Congress 1888-89	
STATES — White	Black	White vote †	Rep. vote	White †	Republican	Democratic	Republican
Virginia	206,248	128,257	102,221	123,080	100	40	4	6
North Carolina	189,732	105,018	114,811	82,393	98	72	7	2
Tennessee	250,055	80,250	125,457	105,856	84	48	8	2
Total	646,035	313,525	342,489	311,329	282	160	19	10
South Carolina	86,900	118,889	39,072	5,960	153	6	7	..
Georgia	177,967	143,471	25,398	1,895	189	30	10	..
Florida	34,210	27,489	33,385	23,152	79	18	2	..
Alabama	141,461	118,423	62,181	24,436	115	18	8	..
Louisiana	108,810	107,977	63,097	21,450	118	16	6	..
Mississippi	108,254	130,278	34,730	10,624	*130	19	6	..
Total	657,602	646,527	257,863	87,517	784	107	39	..

* Legislature 1884-85.
† The assumption is that Negroes all voted Republican. (ED.)
[1] Negroes were to return to the polls in large numbers in the lower South, however, during the Populist revolt in 1892, 1894, and 1896. (ED.)

We also present a similar table for two Northern and two Western states, the wealthiest, most intelligent and most influential of their respective sections. State elections are given because Democrat and Republican, owing to many side parties, do not show total votes:

Males twenty-one and upwards Census 1880		State election 1886	Legislature 1886-87		Congress 1888-89	
STATES	Population	Total votes	Democratic	Republican	Democratic	Republican
New York	1,408,571	970,371	66	94	51	19
Massachusetts	502,648	243,769	93	182	4	8
Ohio	826,577	701,429	58	89	6	15
Illinois	796,827	570,163	87	106	6	14
Total	3,534,623	2,485,732	304	471	67	56

We make a comparison below between the three groups as follows:

Males twenty-one and upwards Census 1880		Percentage of votes 1886		Legislature 1887-88		Congress 1888-89	
STATES	White / Black	Whites	Opposition	Democratic	Republican	Democratic	Republican
Three Southern states ...	646,035 / 313,525	53	100	282	160	19	10
Six Southern states	657,602 / 646,527	39	13	784	107	39	..
Four N. and Western states	3,534,623	70		304	471	67	56

These are suggestive and instructive tables. Leaving out of view altogether the question of intimidation, and granting that there is none, the question is very pertinent whether public affairs are or can be in a healthy or flourishing condition when citizens take so little interest in politics that only thirty-nine per cent of the whites and only thirteen per cent of the blacks voted in the congressional election of 1886.[2] When the citizen cares too little for public affairs to vote, experience proves that matters fall into a deep rut, that abuses multiply, and that government is conducted in the interest of political and corrupt rings, ruled by venal bosses. The South has abundant experience of this fact. The financial officers of Kentucky, Tennessee and Alabama were defaulters to large amounts,[3] and in the financial department of Virginia one treasurer was convicted of stealing, though in a subsequent trial acquitted on the plea of insanity, and two trusted clerks were sent to the penitentiary for robbing — one had continued his robberies for years and to a very large amount, for our treasury watchdogs had been narcotized by the uncontrolled sway of one party and were sound asleep. Uncontrolled party sway inducing indifference on the part of the voter begets favoritism and nepotism, public vices that Jefferson condemned by word and example. Thus in the Virginia capitol there were at one time five, perhaps more, of one family in office, only one of whom was well fitted for his place. They were father (clerk of the Legislature), brother (deputy), son (page), father-in-law, who was about seventy-

[2] Again, voter participation of both races was to increase greatly during the Populist revolt of the 1890's (ED.)

[3] Similar treasury defaications and scandals were exposed in Georgia (1879), Arkansas (1883 and 1890), Louisiana (1889), and Mississippi (1890). (ED.)

five years old when appointed, and brother-in-law (both clerks in auditor's office). The auditor's office, the great financial heart of the state, was presided over by a gentleman whose ability never exceeded that of receiving teller of a bank, and the treasurer, an old gentleman when put in office, was elected by the Legislature on the petition of "had been" endorsed by "sentiment." Of the few deputies appointed by the auditor, one was the old gentleman aforesaid, the old gentleman's son-in-law, another old gentleman who was about seventy-five when appointed, and a clerk, who if not then a thief, was afterwards given full and unlimited authority to rob the state and spend the proceeds in luxurious living. When the healthy and vigorous action of the heart was so impeded and impaired, we can well imagine that the affairs of the state in its various members, the counties, were neither wisely nor faithfully managed. Matters had become so bad that a flood was required to wash them away. General Mahone saw and seized the opportunity, marshaled all the forces in opposition, and soon had almost as undisputed sway as his predecessors previously had.[4] The rotten dead wood was swept aside, and although the new party had many sins, arising principally because its power was also absolute, to answer for, it cannot be fairly claimed that the new order of affairs was worse than the old. We then had so-called Negro rule, but the Commonwealth survived, and, in the opinion of many, was much benefited.

[4] William Mahone (1826-1895), Confederate major general, railroad executive, and leader of the Readjusters, a third-party movement that controlled Virginia politics from 1879 to 1883 and elected Mahone to the United States Senate in 1880. (ED.)

Public affairs can prosper only when all the citizens are enough interested to vote. Compare the wealth, population and influence of Ohio with that of Georgia, already set forth, and see if there may not be some connection therewith in Ohio's vote in 1886 of 701,429 out of a *possible* vote of 826,577 in 1880, and Georgia's vote in 1886 of 27,293 out of a *possible* vote of 321,438 in 1880. The six Southern states[5] instead of rejoicing, as they do, that they have their black fellow-citizens under absolute control, should stimulate all their citizens, white as well as black, for both need stimulation, to take an active and intelligent interest in public affairs, and to show that interest by voting. Competition is not only the life of trade, but competition of parties is the life of the Commonwealth. The only guarantee of continued good government in free countries is an active and intelligent interest in public affairs, and until that interest is excited and shown by a full and free vote, public and private affairs are sure to languish. In Virginia, North Carolina and Tennessee the opposition votes freely, and in 1886 it cast its full strength; but these three states are inferior in no respect to the six other Southern states, but on the contrary are more prosperous and more influential in public affairs. Let the South revert to correct political principles, and she will not suffer, notwithstanding all the dire prophecies we hear from the ruling caste.

But, coming back to the question of intimidation, are the Negroes intimidated and deprived of the ballot, or have they really lost their love of voting? We

[5] I.e., the six states of the lower South named in the table on page 96. (ED.)

cannot say, but certain it is that something has changed their tastes in this respect.

There is said to be a great deal of human nature in the white man, and there probably is a great deal in the Negro, too; but then, again, there may not be, and judging by the difference in his voting in the two groups of states, it is only fair to conclude either that there is very little human nature in some Negroes, or that some Negroes are not human beings. General Henry A. Wise,[6] the distinguished father of the Hon. John S., was of the opinion that Negroes were not human beings, but were Ebo Shins or Gizzard Foots, whatever they may be, though certainly things utterly beneath the regard of the noble Caucasian.

In Virginia the Negro, or Ebo Shin, is infatuated with the ballot, and he seldom lets one pass without casting it. The ballot to him is the epitome of all that is good and noble. It stands in his eyes for deliverance from bondage; for wealth and honor; for public schools and churches; for military and benevolent societies — it stands in his eyes not only for everything he enjoys and hopes to enjoy, but for everything he has escaped. Thus looking upon the ballot, he prizes it above all his other earthly advantages, and when properly led and directed he would on no account forego the privilege of casting his vote. Crops suffering for work will not detain him from the polls, nor fatigue nor illness, unless actually confined to bed, nor even bribes; but, like a well-drilled phalanx, he marches up solidly, and votes solidly, too. Sometimes, of course, apathy overtakes the Negroes

[6] Henry Alexander Wise (1806-1876), Virginia congressman (1833-1844), governor (1856-1860), and Confederate general. (Ed.)

as it does all other parties, and he may then be influenced by many reasons to remain away from the
polls, or to vote with the whites; but let their
leaders get them well in hand, and one had as well
try to stop a stampede of soldiers or animals as to
endeavor to keep them from voting their party ticket.

The ballot also means honor, for thereby he is raised
from his low estate to proud positions of honor, and
he becomes magistrate, assemblyman, congressman,
one of the lawmakers of a great country. Aladdin's
cave itself affords no more enchanting temptation
than does the ballot offer to the Virginia Negro. Yesterday a slave in chains, the ballot today seats him in
the august halls of Congress. Fancy herself nowhere
discloses a more striking transformation, and it is comparable only to nature when it unfolds the brilliant
moth from the hideous grub.

The ballot also means emolument; no, not that, it
means fabulous riches; for the Negro who today may
be sweating in the field for $8.00 a month, or at most
$25.00 or $30.00 as porter, may tomorrow be given
an office worth $1,000 or more a year, or he may be
elected to the Legislature, where in one day he
makes, without labor, almost the wages of a month,
or he may be elected to Congress, where the fabulous
sum of $5,000 a year and perquisites awaits him — and
all by the grace of the ballot. A land flowing with
milk and honey is nothing to these possibilities. It is
like being beside the river Pactolus, where one has
only to stretch out his hands and gather the golden
sands. It is more to him than was Jerusalem to the Jew,
or is Mecca to the Mussulman, or is heaven to the

Christian. Can we marvel, then, that the Negro naturally values the ballot so highly?

In all this the Negro betrays a great deal of human nature, and therefore one must say that the Virginia Negro is a human being; but when we approach the South Carolina or Georgia Negro we are completely mystified, and in spite of our love for all God's creatures, whether man, beast, or fish, we are not prepared to deny any charge that may be brought against the humanity of the Negro of these states. Let us examine this species of Negro. In hair, in color, and in other physical respects he is like the Virginia species, but when we investigate his mental characteristics the resemblance entirely ceases.

A thought here occurs. Science tells us that all nature is merely the creature of its constant surroundings. The Virginia Negro makes tobacco, and has been making it for hundreds of years. The South Carolina and Georgia Negro makes cotton, and has been making it for a century. Now can it be possible that the different environments of tobacco and cotton make all the vast difference that we observe between the two Negroes? It is not only possible, but it *must* be the cause, and he is willfully blind or imbecile who does not see it.

The modern world contends that communities that vote are superior to those that do not vote. Communities being merely citizens in the aggregate, it follows that the Virginia Negroes are superior to the Negroes of South Carolina and Georgia, and it further follows that tobacco elevates and that cotton degrades. Thus it follows further that those who denounce tobacco as the greatest evil except polygamy and whiskey, and those who forbid tobacco-loving preachers exhorting sinners to flee from the wrath to come, are altogether mistaken. The world must change its bearings and its attitude, and instead of anathematizing tobacco, it should preach a crusade in its favor, and should encourage its cultivation and its use, seeing what a great work it has wrought in the elevation of the Virginia Negro. But we must compound for sins we are inclined to by damning those we have no mind to, and as the world must denounce something, let it denounce cotton and renounce its use, seeing the mischief it has wrought with the civic virtues of the South Carolina and Georgia Negroes, who apparently have forgotten that they ever possessed such a thing as a ballot.

But if the tobacco and cotton theory does not satisfy, let us try the theory of religion. The Negro is deeply emotional, and his thoughts dwell much in the spirit land. In his dreams, which are many, and which are not confined to the watches of the night, he, like Jacob, wrestles with the angel, and, like Jacob, he has a ladder resting on his prostrate body and extending into heaven, upon which angels ascend and descend and camp around him.

When walking through the dark shadows of the forest in the deep silence of night, he sees ghosts flitting now before and now behind him, and on his right hand and on his left hand these spiritual beings accompany him. He lives in constant intercourse with the unseeable world, and his prayers are answered literally and speedily. The impenetrable veil that divides us from the so-called "dade" is for him scarcely more than a veil of gauze through which he sees easily, if not clearly. He is a pilgrim and a stranger here; his home is there — in the skies. Here all things are transitory and perishing; there all things are permanent and immortal. The illimitable future and not the finite present, notwithstanding all its carnal delights, which, however, he enjoys so meagerly, is the reality to him.

Now is it not very probable that the South Carolina and Georgia Negro, having such views, cannot interest himself in such worldly matters as elections, and that he does not vote, not because he is intimidated, but because of his intense desire to win the spiritual race that is set before him; and therefore he voluntarily lays aside every weight that besets him, and he fears to vote, lest being embroiled in the snares of political strife and ambition through which he passed for a number of years, he may forget his high calling and thus lose the crown.

The Virginia Negroes, to whom we add the North Carolina and Tennessee Negroes, being the same species, having been elevated, as we have seen, by the cultivation and use of tobacco, prove their claims to humanity by entering boldly the political arena and, though they number only half as many as the whites, by securing for themselves and friends 160 to 282 legislative seats[7] and ten to nineteen congressional seats. But the spiritualized South Carolina Negro, although he numbered in 1880, 118,889 to 86,900 whites, both of voting age, tramples worldly honors and considerations under foot, and reserves for himself and friends only six out of 159 legislative seats,

[7] See the table on page 96.

and he surrenders all the congressional seats. Five thousand dollars a year is no temptation to him, and he prefers his humble cabin, his plain and scanty fare and his small wages, provided he may meekly cultivate the Christian graces and humbly pursue the path to glory. If anybody's soul is to be lost through the wicked wiles and temptations of Washington, he is resolved it shall not be his soul, and he allows without a pang his white brother, who, however, repudiates the relationship, to enjoy those great and worldly prizes. The mighty Cincinnatus achieved imperishable renown by preferring his plow to all the honors and rewards the Mistress of the World could confer, but here is a stranger sight still: thousands of unknown, unheard of, and unsung black Cincinnati renouncing all that this world can confer in order to lead pious lives.

But some will say religion cannot be the cause, for if so, why should the Negroes of Virginia eagerly snatch all the honors and rewards politics can give, while the Negroes of South Carolina despise them all? This is an easy question. The difference is owing simply to the fact that the spirit of Mahone operates in the first group of states, and that the spirit of Sam Jones and Sam Small[8] operates in the other group.

Followers are necessarily like leaders, because leaders are merely the exponents of prevailing sentiment.

Now Mahone, as is well known, is not only unorthodox, but he is also extremely carnal, and seizes all the good things of life without consulting conscience,

[8] Samuel P. Jones (1847-1906), a Southern evangelical minister of the Methodist persuasion, and Samuel W. Small (1851-1915), a popular evangelist and journalist of Georgia, long connected with the Atlanta *Constitution*. (Ed.)

eating what is set before him without asking questions. He refrains from questioning not on account of
scruples but to save time; for if it suited his purposes
he would eat not only the meat offered to idols,
but also the idols themselves.

On the contrary, the two Sams are intensely spiritual. They are forever hunting the devil; they spy him
in every bush, and when found they attack him so
vehemently he ignominiously flies. Repent, renounce
your sins, seek the kingdom of heaven, is their constant refrain; fly for your lives, the devil is right
after you, and if you don't step right lively he has
you sure, and then, oh, my soul, the rest is too frightful to contemplate. Sam Jones has evidently im-
pressed his ideas indelibly upon *all* the people, for
even the whites do not vote, only 25,398 having
voted in Georgia in 1886, although fortunately they
alone enjoy all the public offices. Mahone has demoralized all his Negroes, and Sam Jones has spiritualized all
his. Mahone's Negroes are carnal, and therefore they
clutch at everything within their reach; Sam Jones's
Negroes are thoroughly spiritualized, and they therefore take nothing within their grasp. The fact that the
Negroes of the six [lower] Southern states do not
vote must be attributed solely to the disinterested effects of religion. It cannot be owing to intimidation,
for the whites themselves scarcely vote, and who
intimidates them?

By the way, nobody, we think, can fail from the
foregoing exhibit to be convinced that the Negroes
of the six Southern states are the only true apostolic
Christians now living. Holy Writ teaches us plainly
that we cannot serve God and mammon. To white

Christians this deliverance of divinity has little significance; for, while seeking the kingdom of heaven, they never fail to hold on tightly to all the good things of this world, and instead of entering heaven by prayer, as the good hymn says, and with garments pure and white, they enter it, or think they do, with garments bespotted with groveling tastes and passions, and with the rank odor of earth clinging to them as the smell of musk clings to the vulgarian using it. But to the South Carolina Negroes this injunction is of living force, and, believing they cannot serve two masters, they yield allegiance unreservedly to the higher Master, Christ, and absolutely renounce the world. Thus did the Apostles.

CHAPTER XIII

Why Negro Elevation does not mean Negro Rule — Total Change of Condition between 1865-78 and 1878-88 — Statement of Changed Conditions — If a Free Vote means Negro Rule, then Negro Rule Prevails Over Eastern Virginia — Example of the Black Belt, or Fourth Congressional District in Virginia — A Free Ballot not Injurious to Virginia and Tennessee — Why Negroes are Inimical to Whites — Color Line the Work of Whites — Statesmanship Impossible while Color Line Continues.

But, laying aside badinage and irony, let us say without circumlocution that the Negroes of the six [lower] Southern states are intimidated and deprived of their ballots, for the whites not only acknowledge the fact, but plainly declare and believe that the Negroes should be thus deprived in order to preserve stable and civilized government. If their fears are well grounded, then they are perfectly right in their course; for the first duty of man is to save the state, for a well-governed state is the only soil in which permanent prosperity can flourish. The whites reason as follows: At the close of a four years' war we found ourselves not only thoroughly exhausted, but also completely prostrate at the feet of our enemies. We found the Negroes, everywhere numerous but in many places and in some states in the majority, freed from slavery, and then made citizens; and we found that carpet-baggers and scalawags, by the aid of Negroes naturally crazed with their freedom and its illimitable possibilities, got entire control of state, municipal and county affairs, and by frauds and robberies of every kind made almost a complete wreck of organized society. Because all these dreadful things happened when Federal troops were everywhere, and when a simple lieutenant's sword was weightier and mightier than the voice of any community; when we were completely cowed, and did not know how soon any of us might be arrested and handed over to the military; when the Negroes were totally ignorant and necessarily intoxicated with their freedom; when the passions of war were still active and bitter, and when our conquerors were only too eager to find cause of complaint against us; when the greed of carpet-baggers and the greed and vindictiveness of scalawags and refugee Unionists knew little or no restraint — because such things happened in such a state of affairs (when even worse things might have been apprehended, property and not life having been sacrificed), therefore similar things will happen when the whites are no longer inferiors, suspected and under martial law; when there are no longer carpet-baggers and scalawags to lead the Negroes to their own ruin as well as that of the community; when the Negroes themselves have learned they can never rule the whites, and when, above all, we have all the state governments in our hands, and for years have had at least one branch of the National Government to protect us from unfriendly legislation. To argue thus is to be absolutely illogical — is to be without even the shadow of a foundation to rest upon. To take the ground that having the power we intend to keep it, right or wrong, is easy of comprehension, for we see that the law of the strongest unfortunately still prevails too much everywhere, but for reasonable men to argue that similar results will follow almost totally dissimilar causes is indeed incomprehensible. If modern philosophy agrees on any one point it is on this: that similar effects can result only from similar causes, acting in a similar way on similar objects; change any single one of the conditions and the effects are necessarily different.

Now, are not the conditions of the period from 1865 to the end of the Grant administration and of the period from 1876 to the present different almost as East is from West? And, being so different, how can any man who claims to be reasonable fear a return of the evil days of reconstruction by allowing the Negroes their free right of voting?

Look at a few of the changed conditions:

THEN	NOW
Crushed, demoralized and disorganized.	Confident and disciplined.
Martial law.	Civil law.
Hostile administration and legislature.	Friendly administration and House.

Hostile judiciary and marshals.	Friendly judiciary and marshals.
Hostile state governments and legislatures.	State governments in our absolute control.
Negroes intoxicated with their freedom and unbounded in their anticipations.	Negroes sobered and humbled by experience — wiser.
Carpet-baggers and scalawags in full control.	Carpet-baggers and scalawags things of memory.

To perceive all these changed conditions and to be afraid of a return of former evil days is to prove that we are cowards, not Anglo-Saxons, or, if we are Anglo-Saxons, that we are not worthy of our ancestry; to perceive them and to be unwilling to restore the freedom of the ballot to the Negro is to commit a crime against freedom; and not to see them when they are thrust before our eyes is to prove that we are blind, and that, like blind leaders, we will lead the state into a ditch.

To allow — yea, to encourage — the Negroes to vote freely will not throw the state into the hands of the ignorant and corrupt, though the *personnel* of office-holders will be considerably changed. The most violent of the opponents of Negro suffrage are and will be the office-holding and office-seeking class and their friends, who will cry, "Wolf! Wolf!" and who will frighten most of the majority, composed of well-meaning but timid people.

But we are not left solely to reasoning in this matter, for, fortunately, we have experience to guide us. If the averment prevails that freedom of the ballot for Negroes means Negro rule, then we have Negro rule in the greater portion of Eastern Virginia. Ah! yes; and you are greatly surprised, are you not? For we have conjured up in our minds the idea that Negro rule is some monstrous ogre that remorselessly devours everything that is good and desirable, and that scatters broadcast everything that is bad and baleful, and we cannot discover such a dreadful state of affairs anywhere near us.

But if freedom of ballot means, as is generally asserted, Negro rule, then we must have Negro rule in the greater portion of Eastern Virginia, because nobody claims that the Negroes are intimidated or materially hindered from voting in Virginia, and nobody denies that the Negroes vote solidly for their party. Therefore, if the Negroes have the majority in any counties, and if they are not intimidated, and if they vote solidly for their party, then all counties with Negro majorities must, as a rule, be under Negro rule. Having a majority, not being intimidated from casting that majority, and actually casting that majority freely, there can be no possible escape from the actual fact of Negro rule.

Now, are there any counties in Virginia where Negroes are in the majority? Referring to United States Census 1880, we find there are forty-two counties in Eastern Virginia where the Negroes are in an absolute majority and where, being free to vote, there is consequently Negro rule *in posse* if not *in esse*.

But let us take the example of the fourth congressional district, where the Negro majorities are so large that Negro rule exists not only *in posse*, but also *in esse*.

Thus:

Counties	White	Black
Amelia	3,037	7,340
Brunswick	6,022	10,685
Dinwiddie	14,457	18,428
Greenesville	2,757	5,650
Lunenburg	4,611	6,924
Mecklenburg	8,222	16,388
Nottoway	3,012	8,144
Powhatan	2,726	5,091
Prince Edward	4,754	9,914
Prince George	3,255	6,799
Sussex	3,361	6,701
Total	56,214	102,064

Now, nobody can dispute that if the Negroes are not intimidated, that if they vote freely, and that if, generally, they vote in a solid body, here must be Negro rule; or, if they deny Negro rule here, where else in the South can they possibly fear Negro rule? If nearly two Negroes to one white does not, with a free ballot, constitute Negro rule, then ten Negroes to one white does not mean Negro rule; or if Negro rule is escaped where this proportion of the colors exists, then Negro rule will be escaped anywhere and everywhere in the South. Or if Negro rule does not mean destructive government, where is the sense of representing Negro rule as a return to reconstruction days, when not government but almost anarchy reigned?

If Negro rule means all, or nearly all, the economic, political and social ills, or even partially, that the opponents of Negro suffrage delight so much in picturing, then this fourth congressional district must be in a most lamentable condition — must be a cancerous spot on the fair form of Virginia that saps her whole prosperity. The fourth district may be in this condition, but before deciding let us compare it with the ninth congressional district, a strictly white as the fourth is a strictly black district, which contains per census of 1880: whites, 133,055; blacks, 17,549. Total, 150,604. And with some facts contained in report of auditor of public accounts for the year ending September 30, 1886. The population of the two districts is very nearly the same. Negro rule being the logical and necessary result of unrestricted suffrage, we, of course, find in this fourth district material ruin and moral degradation, and the annual report of the financial officer of the state must show both conditions to prevail, or, if it does not, then the report must be of no value, or those who talk so glibly and so mournfully about Negro rule are false guides and erring prophets.

If the fourth district is ruined financially it can pay no taxes, but the auditor either falsifies the returns or the two districts pay into the state treasury as follows:

	For state	For schools	Total
Fourth District — Black	$74,988	$55,770	$130,758
Ninth District — White	65,609	50,862	116,471

So, then, it would appear that Negro rule, which is synonymous with unrestricted suffrage, does not ruin to such an extent that it cannot contribute its fair share to public burdens and to public schools.

But, then, Negro rule or unrestricted suffrage means official robbery and general demoralization, and perhaps this is the state of affairs in the fourth district, and, if so, the criminal charges ought to be very large. The auditor of the state reports in Table No. 19 the amounts he paid out for such expenses in 1886, and the following comparison is made: fourth district, $22,-173; ninth district, $33,376.

So, then, it would seem that an unrestricted vote and a fair count — or, in other words, Negro rule — render the fourth district not much worse off either financially or morally than the ninth district, where the Negroes are few; and although of late years we hear of little else than of the great boom in Southwest Virginia, it must be confessed that if the figures of our auditor are correct the fourth district is as happy, moral and well off as the great ninth district.

Those who go around wearing the frightful scare-face of Negro rule are doubtless honest in their apprehensions, but they are nevertheless doing an untold amount of evil to the South, which they love well but not wisely.

The fear of Negro rule in the sense of the alarmists is a wild and pernicious chimera, and the experience in the fourth district ought to convince any honest man that it is. The Negro appears to have no ambition to rule, for when he has the majority his almost invaria-ble practice is to give the offices to the most capable white men in his party, and when he cannot get good men from his own ranks he selects worthy Democrats, and remains contented with the crumbs that fall from the official table or with the bones and fragments his white leaders throw him.

The six [lower] Southern states have no more to fear from a free and fair ballot than has the Fourth Virginia District, and if they are wise they will not only permit, but they will encourage, the Negroes to vote; for it is only by inspiring all the people with interest in public affairs that they can expect prosperity. The three states of Virginia, North Carolina and Tennessee, where the opposition cast its full vote in 1886, are no less prosperous than are the six [lower] Southern states where the opposition cast only thirteen per cent of its vote in 1886; but, on the contrary, they exhibit greater progress and prosperity, and certainly as much moral and intellectual development.

The Negroes are against us simply because we treat them not as citizens, but as creatures who have no rights we are bound to respect. But let us respect their rights, and they will gladly co-operate with us. But as long as public affairs are conducted on the color line, which is in reality simply an appeal to passion, prejudice and selfish interests of the lowest kind, the Negroes will remain solid. Wisdom and statesmanship can then have little voice in their management, for the color line deliberately banishes them from the council chamber and the legislature alike.

CHAPTER XIV

Negro not a Competent Voter; neither are Millions of White Voters; but Ballot Absolutely Essential to his Freedom — Ruin of the Commonwealth that Degrades its Citizens — Tyranny Destroys the State and Demoralizes the Citizens — Southerners cannot Escape the Demoralizing Effects of Tyranny.

But the Negro is not a competent voter, and he should never have been entrusted with the ballot. That he is not an intelligent voter in the sense of foreseeing the necessity of wise laws, or of perceiving their bearings on all points, is readily admitted; but, then, who among our millions of white voters, when tested by this standard, are competent? Very few, indeed; and very few of the legislators and congressmen to whom we depute the making of our laws are. But that the Negro, as long as he was not to be a slave, should have the ballot was a matter of absolute necessity; for if he had no ballot to protect his newly acquired freedom, how long could he keep it in the midst of powerful enemies, who regarded him with bitter hostility, because, though once practically supreme master of his time, limb and life, they could not then command his simplest movements? The Negroes would in that case have been literally sheep with wolves for their shepherds. The ballot was, and is, as absolutely essential for freedom as is the atmosphere for life; but let us not fondly imagine that while rendering or seeking to render this right nugatory, and while consequently degrading the Negroes, we are not injuring ourselves.

It is doubtless very gratifying to our baser nature to control absolutely the actions of a whole class of our fellow-creatures; but the enjoyment is suicidal, and it will end in our moral enfeeblement and in our material impoverishment, for ruin must follow communities that persistently degrade any large portion of their citizens. Tyranny, whether national or individual, not only degrades those imposed upon, but it also demoralizes the doers of the wrong, for nobody can deliberately wrong another without feeling humiliated himself, although the constant perpetration of injustice soon renders one callous to the sense of right and wrong. History represents both Nero and Prince Hal as promising youths; but after a while the practice of injustice so changed these fair young men that they became monsters of iniquity and bywords of depravity[1] and so, in a measure, Southerners cannot escape a certain mental and moral obliquity, a certain lowering of the sense of right and wrong, by continuing deliberately to deprive their Negro fellow-citizens of the greatest and most valuable of all their rights — namely, the right of suffrage; and when the moral tone is lowered all their undertakings must necessarily be injuriously affected thereby.

[1] Neither legend nor history, of course, would support such a comparison. (ED.)

History is one long record of the fact that privilege, whether founded on brute force and stamped only on the fickle mind of the unbridled savage or cruel despot, or whether deeply imprinted on the social mind in the guise of unyielding caste, or whether crystallized in deliberate laws upon the statute book, has this dual effect of degrading and debasing the lower and of demoralizing and finally of debasing the higher, the grand finale being the stagnation or destruction of the State; and can the South expect to escape such consequences if it persists in maintaining its practical oligarchy (all oligarchies have been short-lived), whereby, though all are alike in the contemplation of law, at least half the population of six [lower South] states is practically deprived of the most sacred right of freemen — the right freely to declare its voice at the polls.

If the South desires prosperity it must, granting that the Negroes are not intimidated, encourage them to take interest in public affairs, and to show their interest by voting; and granting that the Negroes are intimidated, it is our double duty to put a stop to the suicidal practice, for in these days of active competition the South needs the active and intelligent co-operation of all its citizens in order to prosper, but if by intimidation we cripple the hopes and ambition of half the people who are our principal dependence for labor, we have nothing to hope for but disaster. As well hamstring a horse or mule and expect work from it as to expect valuable results from degraded and hopeless labor.

But the Negro has all his rights — let him use them. Yes, he has them nominally, but the principal one, the ballot, is held pretty much on the following tenure:

An officer on one occasion called for volunteers from his assembled command for some desperate work. He invited all who were unwilling to volunteer to step to the front, but he added, with a Sheridan oath, that he would shoot the first man that did so. If one is to be slain for not volunteering, he prefers to go along and take chances; and so the Negro thinks that if he is to be intimidated and even killed for exercising his nominal rights, he had better forego them altogether.

The South will look in vain for prosperity as long as it abridges the right of voting of any class of its citizens.

CHAPTER XV

Education — Its Vast Importance — Sums Spent Annually by Ohio, Michigan, Indiana, and Illinois — Tables of Non-Readers and Non-Writers in Eleven Southern States — Of the Press South and other States — Of Higher Education — Many Lawyers, but Few Mechanical, Scientific, or Literary Men in Southern States.

We have now come to the subject of education which, from its great importance, we must treat at some length.

In these modern days, while there are many different ideas as to methods of education, there are no two opinions as to the value and importance — nay, as to the necessity — of education itself, and so strongly is this necessity felt in many parts of the Union, for instance in the central states of Ohio, Michigan, Indiana and Illinois, that they spend vast sums for educational purposes, averaging annually, according to the United States Bureau of Education, very nearly $30,000,000, which is an average of $10 for each of their children between seven and nineteen years of age, or about $20 for each child actually attending school.

As education is the great lever that moves the world, it is of vital importance to the prosperity and influence of any country that this lever should be in good condition; for now, if ever, knowledge is power and wealth too, and education is the parent of knowledge. The South is no exception to this general law; she holds no dispensation whereby ignorance may do the work of knowledge, and if she desires prosperity and influence, she, too, like the rest of the world, must encourage education. Let us now see what is the condition of education within her bounds.

We will first take the children of ten years of age and upwards, and divide them into readers and non-readers:

STATES	Census of 1880: ten years and upwards Can read	Census of 1880: ten years and upwards Cannot read	Percentage of readers to non-readers
Alabama	481,501	370,279	
Arkansas	378,647	153,229	
Florida	114,431	70,219	
Georgia	597,157	446,683	
Louisiana	351,758	297,312	
Mississippi	438,081	315,612	
North Carolina	592,061	367,890	
South Carolina	345,676	321,780	
Tennessee	767,745	294,385	
Texas	807,973	256,223	
Virginia	698,539	360,495	
Total	5,573,569	3,254,107	63 37

The proportion in the four Western states already referred to, of readers to non-readers, is 95 ¾ to 4¼.

The following shows those of ten years and upwards of the whites who cannot write:

STATES	Census of 1880		Percentage of writers to non-writers: whites
	Can write	Cannot write	
Alabama	340,955	111,767	
Arkansas	295,363	98,542	
Florida	79,374	19,763	
Georgia	435,043	128,934	
Louisiana	261,966	58,951	
Mississippi	274,848	53,448	
North Carolina	416,774	192,032	
South Carolina	212,931	59,774	
Tennessee	574,517	216,227	
Texas	685,015	123,912	
Virginia	515,892	114,692	
Total	4,092,678	1,178,042	77⅔ 22⅓

These two tables give a clear official view of the condition of general education in the South in 1880, and it is not believed that there has been any very great improvement since then, except in the cities.

We will now give two tables, showing the state of what may be called public intelligence and of the higher walks of cultivation. First in importance comes the press. The following table is from census of 1880:

STATES	Dailies	All other periodicals	Circulation	
			Dailies	All others
South	128	1,612	196,533	1,504,424
Other states	843	9,702	3,369,862	26,708,867

Rowell's Newspaper Directory for 1887 gives:

STATES	Dailies	Weeklies	Monthlies
South	156	1,631	152
Other states	1,155	9,485	1,503

Rowell gives no estimate of aggregate circulation, but he represents only one Southern paper as having a daily circulation exceeding 15,000, only three exceeding 10,000, only four exceeding 7,500, only three exceeding 5,000, and only three exceeding 4,000.

As showing higher education, the following is taken from report of United States Commissioner of Education for 1884-85: number of university and college students in the South, 6,486; in other states, 27,891. This is a better showing as regards numbers, but we can judge better as to the quality of instruction when we remember there is only one Southern university of national reputation — namely, the University of Virginia, while the other states have Yale, Harvard, Princeton, Cornell, Johns Hopkins, Stevens Institute of Technology, and others that attract students from all parts of the United States.

As further showing the condition of higher cultivation in the South, it must be borne in mind that though we had and still have many men distinguished in law, medicine and politics, we have had and still have very few men noted in mechanics, science, art, literature, invention.

As bearing also on this point, an examination of Johnson's Encyclopaedia, an American work of standard authority, shows that only one editor, A. H. Stevens, out of thirty-one, was Southern, and only thirty out of 730 writers on special subjects were Southern, among whom were Beauregard, Lamar, Hampton, Curry.[1] There were thousands of other contributors, of whom the South doubtless supplied some, but the names of these sub-writers are not given. It is not to be expected that a large proportion of contributors would be Southern, but the fact of so exceedingly few having been engaged may well prove a great dearth of higher education.

Having now given a very general and cursory, but not, it is believed, an unfair or inaccurate survey of the state of education in the South, let us now look at the subject more in detail, so that we may accurately perceive the conditions and the difficulties surrounding the question, because until we get this view we will not be in a situation to take the essential steps to disseminate education among *all* the people.

[1] Pierre Gustave Toutant Beauregard (1818-1893); Lucius Quintus Cincinnatus Lamar (1825-1893); Wade Hampton (1818-1902); Jabez Lamar Monroe Curry (1825-1903). (Ed.)

CHAPTER XVI

Education Continued — Private and Voluntary, or Public and Compulsory, Schools only Methods of Combatting Ignorance — South Dependent on Wretched Public Schools — Tables of School Population and Number to Square Mile in Southern States and in Four Western States — Number of Square Miles Required for Average School of Thirty — Percentage of School Attendance — Average Pay of School Teachers and Average Day's Attendance in South — With Separate Schools Education Impossible and Prosperity a Delusion.

If education is not a prerequisite of progress and prosperity, or if among all the people sixty-three readers to thirty-seven non-readers, or if among the whites alone seventy-eight writers to twenty-two non-writers, is not a bad condition of education, then this whole question of education drops, and there is nothing more to be said; but if education is a necessity of progress and prosperity, if among all the people of ten years and upwards sixty-three readers to thirty-seven non-readers, and among the whites seventy-eight writers to twenty-two non-writers, be a deplorable state of affairs, then a practical and pressing problem of the greatest and gravest magnitude confronts us, and the question is, How shall we meet and solve it? There are only two ways — namely, private and voluntary, or public and compulsory, schools. If all could afford the expense of private schools, so that every neighborhood, however sparsely settled, could have a good school, private schools would undoubtedly be the best means of education, because they are flexible and can be easily accommodated to local and personal conditions; but the poverty of the South utterly precludes all possibility of such a system, and therefore we are necessarily thrown back upon public schools, with all their rigidity, where children are stretched figuratively upon procrustean beds and cut off or stretched out to accommodate them to their inflexible system. Public schools have now taken the place of the Pharisee's Sunday, men being supposed to be made for Sunday and not Sunday for men, and so children are now made for public schools and not public schools for children. But whatever their faults, we are confined to public schools and must accommodate ourselves to them.

The conditions found in the South are poverty, sparseness of population, great ignorance; and the forces to meet and overcome these conditions are indifferent public schools. But such schools, which must necessarily continue indifferent, will never answer, and our only hope is good public schools; and the question of how to get good public schools is the one we have to solve. In default of money, there is only one way, and that is a large clientage of pupils, for without many scholars there cannot be sufficient financial basis to secure good teachers, and without good teachers good public schools are an absolute impossibility. Now let us see our basis for this large clientage. We will take the census of 1880 for our guide, and we will include all children from seven to nineteen years of age, which gives us a school period of thirteen years. We find by experience that an enrollment of fifty is requisite to secure average attendance of thirty. We therefore calculate on the basis of enrollment of fifty.

STATES	Children 7 to 19		Area (square miles)	Black 7 to 19 Square miles	White 7 to 19 Square miles	School of 30	
	White	Black				Square miles (white)	Square miles (black)
Alabama	197,507	193,054	52,250	3.75	3.69	13.33	13.55
Arkansas	179,137	64,413	53,850	3.33	1.20	15.00	41.66
Florida	41,759	38,862	58,580	0.71	0.66	70.42	75.75
Georgia	240,596	232,955	59,475	4.06	4.05	12.31	12.31
Louisiana	135,503	141,932	48,720	2.80	2.90	17.14	17.24
Mississippi	144,078	209,044	46,810	3.08	4.45	16.23	11.00
North Carolina	252,510	171,604	52,250	4.83	3.28	10.35	15.24
South Carolina	112,447	189,968	30,570	3.67	6.21	13.62	8.05
Tennessee	354,844	131,025	42,050	8.44	3.12	5.93	16.00
Texas	349,393	129,725	265,780	1.31	0.49	38.16	102.00
Virginia	256,991	202,203	42,450	6.05	4.76	8.26	10.50

As a companion table, the following is given:

STATES	Children 7 to 19	Area (square miles)	Children 7 to 19 Square miles	School of 50 Square miles
Illinois	920,304	56,650	16.25	3.08
Indiana	609,826	36,350	16.77	2.98
Michigan	452,597	58,915	7.68	6.51
Ohio	930,866	41,050	22.67	2.25

When we look at the first of these two tables we will hardly be surprised at our illiteracy, when we see that the two most thickly populated States, namely, Virginia and Tennessee, required an area respectively of 8.26 and 5.93 square miles for a white school of thirty scholars, and that Georgia, the Empire and model State, required 12.31 square miles, provided every white child and youth between seven and nineteen actually attended school at some period of the year.

But this difficulty of clientage is much increased when we take not the actual number of children — for very many of these have not begun school by seven, and very many more have left school before nineteen — but the enrollment and average attendance. Thus:

STATES	Children 7 to 19	United States Bureau of Education Report of 1884-85		Percentage of attendance to whole population
		Enrollment	Average attendance	
Alabama	390,561	233,909	144,572	11.45
Georgia	473,551	291,505	195,035	12.65
North Carolina ..	424,114	298,166	185,578	13.26
Virginia	459,194	303,343	176,469	11.66

Applying the above percentage, which is actual experience, we find that only four years ago it required the following square miles respectively for white schools of thirty scholars: 20.55, 17.44, 13.71, 12.40. The number of thirty scholars is selected, as already stated, because any less number would not afford sufficient grading of pupils or compensation of teachers to make good schools.

Now, here is a physical impediment which can be overcome only by a large increase of population, and what prospect is there of this increase? Very little indeed, for except in some of our few cities, and in several accessible mining regions, where the increase is noteworthy, the agricultural sections, which are the real South, are not much more than holding their own in numbers. In order to have the school basis of Indiana and Illinois, the states of Alabama and Georgia must more than quadruple their white population, North Carolina must increase hers three and a half times, and Virginia must increase hers two and three-fourths fold.

The other Southern states, except Tennessee, are not so favorably situated as the four already cited.

What is the prospect in this, or the next, or even in the third generation, of this increase, or of anything like it?

And what, in the meantime, is to become of the education of the people? The bulk of the white population will necessarily remain uneducated, and many must continue illiterate, and the states must inevitably fall behind in the race of prosperity and progress; and lacking in prosperity, they will as inevitably fall under the dominion of the other states of the Union.

Therefore, instead of increasing greatly in population, we may esteem ourselves fortunate if, in our ignorant condition, we be not deserted by the flower of our youth, attracted by prosperity elsewhere, and we thus be unable to hold our present numbers; and little or no increase of population taking place, there will be little if any improvement in our public schools.

According to the report of the United States Bureau of Education, the South spent in one year $8,475,-993.00 for education, and we may continue for years to spend this vast sum annually, but it will be almost entirely thrown away in the country at large until we have a large enough white population to furnish children enough for schools, large and frequent enough and kept up long enough to attract an ample supply of competent teachers. Without good subaltern officers an army is little better than a mob; so without good teachers schools are little better than a mockery.

The following table shows the wretched implements our public school teachers must necessarily be, for they do not average the compensation of housemaids, who are likewise boarded, and shows how little schooling the children receive:

STATES	Average annual pay of teachers: Census of 1880	Average school days. United States Com. of Education, 1884-85
Alabama	$ 83.70	82.04
Arkansas	117.52	Not given
Florida	86.16	95.
Georgia	100.25	Not given
Louisiana	217.79	110.
Mississippi	119.37	78.05
North Carolina	52.46	62.
South Carolina	96.20	70.
Tennessee	106.88	80.
Texas	105.54	100.
Virginia	145.17	118.40

To fight the battle of education with our present forces and present system of separate schools seems well-nigh hopeless. But what shall we do? Shall we go on in our past and present wasteful and inefficient manner; shall we keep on and spend the little money we have and get small benefit from it, except in the cities and larger villages, or shall we look around for reinforcements in order to contend successfully with ignorance? If education is an essential of progress and prosperity, we must do it; and if we value education properly, we will search anxiously for these reinforcements; and if we only *will* it we shall gain our end, for the old adage is still true, "Where there is a will there is a way." But they are not to be procured by wishes or even by prayers, but only by action, and by action, too, that will clash with all of our preconceived ideas, that will be distasteful and repugnant to our prejudices, but not to reason and justice. But if we are serious in our desires for prosperity, we will not let them deter us, for to stumble and falter at things that are distasteful and repugnant is at once to put a stop to all progress — physical, moral and intellectual — for what in reality is progress but the overcoming of prejudice and hostility?

The rise and triumph of Christianity itself was simply an overcoming of the violent prejudices and repugnances of the civilized world; and, in truth, all reforms, and the more beneficial the reform the greater generally are the obstructions to be overcome, are contests against, and finally victories over, what is distasteful and repugnant. Volumes, and exceedingly interesting ones, too, could be written about reforms gained in spite of what was distasteful, and of reforms yet delayed, but still to come, because of distaste and repugnance, active and violent or phlegmatic, but deep-seated. To say, therefore, that our reinforcements are distasteful and repugnant is really to say nothing against them, and is no reason why we, if wise, should reject them. Our interest is to examine these reinforcements and see if they will be efficient aids to escape from our great and deplorable ignorance, and if found to be feasible and practical, and especially if found to be essential, we should embrace and set them in motion without delay. Our impulse will be to say: impossible, or the thing shall never be done; but we should be very chary of saying anything is impossible, or that such a thing shall never be, in view of what has taken place and in view of what we have agreed to in the past quarter-century. In that time we have seen slaves made freedmen at the scratch of one man's pen; by a simple "Be it enacted" we have seen freedmen made citizens, legislators, jurors, teachers of youth, etc., etc.; we have seen civil and political society completely changed, and social life profoundly modified; in a word, we are living in a new world, and we have assented to all these fundamental changes that have made the new world.

Now, no changes in the future can ever be so radical as those of the past, and therefore we should never again say anything is impossible, or that we shall never permit it, until after we have given the subject a fair, deliberate and impartial consideration. And so, in the remedy proposed to educate our people, we should, in our own interest, hear calmly and fairly before striking. If what is proposed is impracticable, condemn it and let it perish; but if it is necessary and feasible, even though very hard and difficult, we may be sure that time will bring the end about in spite of any opposition we may make; or that if we persistently refuse, Southern society must continue to lie not only in a bed of ignorance, but of poverty, too.

CHAPTER XVII

Education Continued — Remedy Proposed — The Abandonment of Separate Schools — The Necessity Thereof and Why — It Doubles Basis for Schools — Separate Schools a Public Proclamation of Caste — Inferiority of Negroes — Why They Render General Education Impossible — Their Tendency Radically Demoralizing — Differences between Men Principally Differences of Education.

The remedy proposed is not a bread pill or some soothing syrup, but is a radical and far-reaching one, and is no less than the abandonment of the principle of separate schools, which principle is an efficient and certain mode of dooming to perpetual ignorance both whites and blacks in thinly settled sections.

This remedy will, of course, as already said, be extremely distasteful, and will be violently opposed unless its necessity and its advantages can be demonstrated, for until this is done the whites will never consent to co-education, but will prefer to remain ignorant. We will, then, endeavor to show the necessity and the advantage.

The necessity for the abandonment of separate

schools is dual — physical and moral. The physical necessity is this: With our sparse population separate schools cannot supply a clientage numerous enough to secure good teachers, upon whom the efficiency of the public schools is absolutely dependent, but the abandonment of separate schools at once doubles the school population in the South at large, and at once furnishes a basis upon which good public schools can be built. Thus, South Carolina, instead of 3.67 white children, has 9.88 of all children to the square mile; Georgia, instead of 4.06, has 8.11, and Virginia, instead of 6.05, has 10.81, etc., ample enough basis for good public schools.

The moral necessity is this: Separate schools are a public proclamation to all of African or mixed blood that they are an inferior caste, fundamentally inferior and totally unfit to mingle on terms of equality with the superior caste. That this is not a temporary and ephemeral but a fundamental and caste inferiority is proven by the fact that opposition does not cease when the temporary inferiority ceases, but still operates, however cultured and refined the Negro may be. Hence it follows that separate schools brand the stigma of degradation upon one-half of the population, irrespective of character and culture, and crush their hope and self-respect, without which they can never become useful and valuable citizens. Life is hard enough and progress is slow enough with all the tonic of self-respect and with all the stimulus of hope, but deprived thereof, the boldest and the bravest among the whites cease effort and relapse into despondency, despair or recklessness; but when we make our implement of elevation, namely our public schools, simply a branding iron for stamping the letter "D," degraded, upon the foreheads of millions of black fellow-citizens, we deliberately tear up by the roots all our other efforts for their amelioration. We can improve the beauty, strength, speed and usefulness of animals by careful feeding, housing and training, but we can never make men of human beings simply by attending, however carefully, to their physical neces- sities — meat and drink of the best quality and in the greatest abundance leave them animals still. We can only make men of them by cultivating and stimulat- ing their higher and nobler natures, their mental and moral parts, and this can never be done while the principle of separate schools remains in full force.

We can never stamp out illiteracy in the South at large as long as this principle is closely followed, for it requires that if there are not whites enough to form a separate school, then all such must remain igno- rant, and if not enough blacks to form a separate school, then all the blacks must remain ignorant; and as these conditions are found everywhere in the South, general ignorance of course follows. In cities, large villages, and populous neighborhoods, separate schools may very well, as a matter of convenience, just as in the case of segregation of the sexes, where co-equality is acknowledged, be kept up, provided, however, that no children are on account of color excluded from convenient schools and forced to attend inconvenient schools; but if they are, then separate schools be- come an engine of degradation.

If we could arrange matters, we would be some- what like the preacher of a New England fishing vil- lage in his prayers for favorable winds for the fishing smacks. If he prayed for fair winds for those going fishing, he necessarily prayed for bad wind for those returning from fishing. So what does he do? Not wishing of course to offend any of his flock, he beseeches the Almighty for a fresh but not violent *side* wind. So if we had the management of, or if prayers prevailed in, the school realm, there should be just enough of each color in every neighborhood to form a good school, and the homes should be so situated that each color would find it most convenient to attend its own school, and then everything would be lovely, because, in colloquial phrase, "The goose would then honk high."

But, alas, we have not the management, and people will locate themselves where there are sure to be either too many or not enough of each color; and, under the system of separate schools, thousands and hundreds of thousands must remain without instruction, and what are we going to do about it? Oblivious of the fact that the whites must through this system be very great sufferers, if not the greatest, because they have most to lose, and looking only at the despised blacks, old ideas and old ways oppose every change, for they really care very little whether the blacks ever become better than field hands in the country or bootblacks and menials in the city.

But good sense and justice are not blinded by prejudice or prescription, and are keenly alive to the fact that not only is knowledge the parent of virtue, but that ignorance is the mother of depravity; and they know that it is the ignorant generally who become food for the brothels, jails and penitentiaries, who are the main supporters and upholders of saloons and barrooms, and who fill most of the drunkards' graves, and who are the depredators upon the labors of the industrious. Good sense and justice say, their parents pay taxes and their children are therefore entitled to instruction, and they say further that even if their parents do not pay taxes, it is a shame to humanity and an injury to society to let any of these little ones grow up ignorant and untrained; and after the manner of One who was the incarnation of justice and good sense, as well as of mercy, they say to all the little ones, white and black alike, "Come unto us," and those whom separate schools would make outcasts they take in their arms and carry to school, where they will be taught to know right from wrong and trained to practice what they learn.

Justice and good sense proclaim that education is sight to the blind, hearing to the deaf, feet to the lame, and strength to the weak; that it is the one pearl of great price, and that as the husbandman in Scripture sold all that he had in order to procure it, so every people, so we of the South, should sacrifice means, prejudices, antipathies — everything, if necessary, so that all our children may be educated; for if we should have lost all and gained education, we are then in position to regain more than we have lost; but if we should have saved all and lost education, then, like the fool who had gained the world and lost his soul, we, through ignorance and illiteracy, will finally lose all that we were fondly imagining that we were saving. The differences between man and man are principally the difference of education. Bismarck an untutored savage would be the bold and cruel leader of some bloodthirsty horde; Bismarck educated is the ruling spirit of Europe's greatest empire, and all the nations of the old world hang breathless upon his slightest political utterance.

Certain things cannot coexist. In classic times it was Rome or Carthage, with Patrick Henry it was liberty or death, and in the late war it was slavery or freedom; and so now justice and good sense proclaim that separate schools and general education cannot coexist. To say, when other portions of the country have in a great measure condemned separate schools, that we cannot rise to the occasion when the prize is the redemption of our country from the disgrace and curse of ignorance, is to belittle and dishonor ourselves.

CHAPTER XVIII

Education Continued — Fear of Demoralization — Mixed Schools do not Mean Demoralization of Whites but Elevation of Blacks. Influence Descends — The Higher Demoralizes the Lower, not the Lower the Higher — Example of Nurses — Of Playmates — The Mammy — Examples of Higher Demoralizing Lower.

But while thousands are sincerely desirous of doing full justice to the Negro, they yet cling to separate schools because of a dread of demoralization, which they fancy is inseparable from mixed schools. Because they sometimes see degraded white men mix with Negroes they imagine they have been demoralized by the association, though the fact is they did not mingle with the blacks until they had become demoralized, and they therefore imagine that the simple mingling of the two colors in the same school, however guarded and however well regulated the public schools were, would also cause demoralization. In this they are thoroughly illogical, for besides forgetting that reputable colored people will not mingle with degraded whites, they also overlook the fact that from earliest childhood they have been subjected to intimate Negro association, and yet they have not been degraded; and if they were not demoralized by the unrestrained influences of Negro nurses at the very time the mind and the heart are most susceptible to influence of every kind, why should they fear demoralization for their children when under the well-guarded restraint of well-managed public schools? They can have no well-grounded apprehension, and such fears are chimerical. Moreover, they should bear in mind that influence, whether demoralizing or elevating, is like the rain — it descends. The higher ranks of society elevate or demoralize the lower, but rarely do the virtues or the vices of the lower affect the higher one way or the other; and in the mingling of the two colors in the public schools the result would necessarily be not the degradation of the higher but the elevation of the lower. It is impossible to conceive of well-bred children preferring, to any extent, the bad habits and language of unkempt and untrained little Negroes. Instead of being attracted, they will be repelled by every manifestation of bad ways, bad language, and bad thoughts, just as the virtues of Spartan children were invigorated by witnessing the vices of helots. Even in separate schools, both private and public, children do not form many intimate acquaintances, and in mixed schools there is little likelihood of white children forming any intimacies with black children. It will not of course be so agreeable to attend mixed as separate schools, but when it is narrowed down to almost no good schools for a great part of the South, or good mixed schools, it would seem to be the height of folly to allow feeling or sentiment to rob us of the inestimable blessings of education. Purists such as these ought not to enter rail cars if they saw Negroes therein, or they should get out as soon as they saw one enter, and should walk to their destination or return home, and after they get home they should remain there, lest they be demoralized by even the sight of a black skin. People and their children so susceptible to contamination should not have Negro cooks or maids, Negro butlers or coachmen, for if education in well-regulated public schools will engender demoralization, then servants who come into close daily contact with master and mistress, with young Master John and young Miss Mary, will surely bestrew their paths with frightful white moral wrecks.

If mere association in well-regulated public schools, where bad children will be closely watched or expelled, will cause demoralization, what an opportunity the "mammy" had to put in her deadly work. Most of us above thirty years of age had our mammy, and generally she was the first to receive us from the doctor's hands, and was the first to proclaim, with heart bursting with pride, the arrival of the fine baby. Up to the age of ten we saw as much of the mammy as of the mother, perhaps more, and we loved her quite as well. The mammy first taught us to lisp and to walk, played with us and told us wonderful stories, taught us who made us and who redeemed us, dried our tears and soothed our bursting hearts, and saved us many a well-deserved whipping; nursed us kindly and faithfully in sickness, and if death, in spite of all, snatched away a little cherub, she mingled her tears without reproof with those of the mother. The mother might grow weary and faint, but the faithful mammy seemed never to weary, but was always patiently and lovingly at her post, and when her summons came to go up higher we laid her tenderly to rest. In the hands of the Negro mammy we were as clay to the potter, but did she demoralize us? Thousands who are scattered over the land, and in whose memory the mammy holds a tender and an honored place, have but one response, "No."

And when we became youths and played with Negro boys, went fishing and hunting with them, gathered berries and nuts together, climbed the same trees, and threw down apples and cherries to the girls and little boys whose legs were too short to grasp the trees; and when we became older, young men and maidens, and had colored body-servants and colored maids, who were constantly at our elbow and who knew all our love affairs, etc., became we then demoralized? No; and why? For the simple reason that we were higher, and the higher are rarely, if ever, demoralized by the lower. Influence descends, and if we mingle in the same schools the whites will not be demoralized, because they are the higher, the nobler, the richer; but the blacks through the influence of the whites will be elevated. The danger of contamination will not be from black but from bad white children, for the latter will have constant and easy access to all, while the former will be naturally confined to association with their own color. For centuries the Southern whites have been intimately associated with the blacks, and have we become demoralized? And if not we can have no well-grounded fears of contamination from well-regulated public schools.

When the writer hears the cry of demoralization,

born as he has been and lived as he has in Southern society, and knowing intimately its dark as well as its bright side, he can only smile and recall the old fable of the lamb muddying the wolf's drinking water. The morals of the blacks are bad, and they are doubtless very glad to receive the impure advances of the whites, but as a rule they are not the tempters but the tempted; they are passive, and if they are not sought by the whites they will rarely seek the latter. History, fiction, the drama, everyday life, all abundantly illustrate the demoralizing effects of the higher upon the lower walks of society. Books furnish thousands of instances, as we read in *David Copperfield* and *Adam Bede*, of the higher male destroying the virtue of the humble female, and although we hear sometimes of grooms marrying their masters' daughters, we have to hunt a very long time to find one instance of the lower male seducing the higher female; and so it is in the South in the intercourse of the two colors. The virtue of the white female is secured by the ease with which the higher white debauches the lower black. Demoralization, indeed! If the prophet Nathan were now alive, and were to be as plainspoken as he was in David's time, few Southern men would dare, in his presence, to cry demoralization, lest he should point his finger at him and say, Thou art the man.

CHAPTER XIX

Other Injurious Consequences of Separate Schools and Other Advantages of Mixed Schools — Separate Schools Mean Oligarchy, Caste, and not Democracy — Inculcate Inequality at Beginning of Instruction, Cultivate Autocracy and Haughtiness in Whites and Abasement and Servility in Blacks — Emancipation, Negro Suffrage, Negroes on Juries, etc., etc., proved Chimeras; so will Mixed Schools — Mixed Schools will Disseminate Correct Ideas of Liberty.

If we, as a people, are to be democratic and not oligarchic, and if, as individuals, we are to be all equal and not some superiors and some inferiors, it must be not through means of separate schools, but through schools whose doors freely open to all within the school district; but if we are not to be democratic, if there are to be permanent classes or castes among us, some of whom enjoy privileges denied to others — in other words, if we are to change our whole theory of government — then separate schools based on color or caste are the most effective means we can employ.

For as already said, separate schools are a public proclamation to the blacks that they are *so* degraded that no improvement of mind, morals, manners and appearance will ever fit them for admission to white schools; that a gulf as impassable as that between Dives and Lazarus separates them from the whites, impossible of being crossed by the blacks because the whites forbid, and impossible of being crossed by the whites because caste, the most cruel, the most odious, the most blind of all the devices of man to secure selfish advantage, forbids. Separate schools poison at its very source the stream whence spring the best and noblest fruits of education, because at the very beginning of instruction the little ones are taught two dogmas — first, that white children are and shall *forever* be fundamentally superior to black children; and, second, that black children are and *forever* shall be fundamentally inferior to white children. At the fountain of education the doctrine of caste, which elsewhere is being successfully combatted, is enshrined in fresh vigor and authority, and it seizes with its rigid, icy grasp the impressible minds of the children, and taints them; and the blind superiority thereby inculcated fosters sentiments of false pride, disregard of the rights of others, and unfeeling haughtiness to all, regardless of color, whom they deem inferiors; and the inferiority thereby taught the blacks cultivates feelings of abasement and of servile fear of all whom they consider superior — sentiments totally destructive of manliness, courage and self-respect, the noblest jewels in the character of man.

Separate schools are necessarily injurious to both colors. To the black they are a deliberate affront, and their tendency is to keep the whole Negro population in a degraded condition; and they likewise tend to deteriorate the character of the whites, for they make of them oligarchs, priding themselves not on their merits but on their status, despising all below them, and contemning labor because labor is performed by menials and inferiors.

But mixed schools, which at first blush we so much dread, are not half so shocking or so bad as were Negro emancipation, Negro voting, Negro lawmaking, Negroes sitting on juries, Negroes riding in rail and street cars, our lordly selves standing the meanwhile, Negroes sleeping in the same berths on Pullman cars, etc., etc.; but where is our dread of them? Dissipated by experience. And what will become of our dread of mixed schools? That, too, will be proved equally chimerical. The rearing of our children will have been very defective, and their virtues will be very feeble and sickly, if they will be demoralized by the Negro children; and if they should be, it would only prove that white parents had been extremely negligent in raising their offspring; but they will not be demoralized. On the other hand, however, their fine appearance, their good breeding, and their virtuous ways will be constant bright examples which the black children will be continually imitating, and instead of bad manners, bad morals and bad language spreading among our children, good language, good morals and good manners will spread among the black children. Entirely separated as the two races now are during education, the black children, not having the high white model constantly before their eyes, generally consider it a small disgrace to be ragged and dirty, to be vulgar and profane, to lie and to steal; and only after they come in contact with their betters during school hours can we expect very material improvement; but when this is done we may confidently look for a vast improvement in their dress, speech, habits and ways.

Another and incalculable advantage of mixed schools will be that the whites will be taught the valuable lesson needed to be learned by every citizen of a free country, that the difference between man and man is not color, but character and conduct — worth makes the man; want of it, the fellow, saith the poet — and when this lesson is thoroughly learned, then will be disarmed that baleful pride that leads them to regard themselves as superior simply by virtue of a lighter skin, and which teaches them that it is needless to attempt excellence by the acquisition of virtue and knowledge; for why labor and strive to excel when they already excel without toilsome effort? When children are taught, as separate schools practically do, that superiority consists in a white skin, they will naturally be satisfied with that kind of superiority, and they will not willingly undergo the tedious, painful and patient ordeal requisite to prepare them for superiority in science, art, literature — in all the vast range of attainments which make us to differ from our savage and barbarous ancestors.

One reason, most likely, why the South has always shown, and still shows, so little intellectual development, apart from law and politics, is that the whites have been possessed of the idea that the height of superiority is a white skin, and that they have been content with that kind of eminence. Mixed schools will, in time, emancipate us from this fallacy; but until they do, or are in a fair way of doing so, it will be vain to look for much indigenous intellectual vitality in the South, and most of what may develop will be compelled to seek, as in the past, its encouragement in communities where ideas of human equality have fair play, and where they are not throttled by caste. There are many Southern men of capacity and influence in the North and West, either attracted or forced there because they had no field or no intellectual liberty in their native land. It is not that Southern intellect is any way inferior to intellect anywhere else, only in the South its exercise and development are cribbed, cabined and confined by inexorable caste.

CHAPTER XX

The Color Line — Dangers of this Line — Who Draws It, Whites or Blacks? — Whites Opposed to Every Right Gained by Blacks, and Refuse them All Office — Blacks when in Control Confer Offices on Whites — Why Blacks Vote for Republicans and Against Democrats.

Lines of demarkation in the social body, if attended with enmity, are always injurious, because then the efforts of the people, instead of being directed to the general good, are turned against each other.

The theological line, now happily almost extinct, has in its day wrought incalculable evil, irretrievably injuring some countries, which still seem to lag superfluous upon the stage of nations, and has absolutely destroyed great empires once happy, rich and prosperous, but now deserted and desolate wildernesses.

The race and other lines have also in their day wrought untold havoc, and in recent days and smaller spheres the Know-Nothing line, the Knights of Labor line, the Sectional line, and many other lines have joined forces in working injury, enormous in the aggregate, to the welfare and happiness of men.

Another line, sharply dividing the social structure, has of recent years become painfully prominent, and is now grimly confronting us, and that line is —

THE COLOR LINE,

a line certain to be most pernicious to our prosperity, if it cannot, like the religious line, be obliterated.

This line is at present deep, black and broad, and almost as impassable as that separating Lazarus and Dives; and if nothing can be done to remove it, then Ichabod, like a royal cipher, must be stamped on most things Southern, for this line, as long as its dark shadow menaces us, means perpetual discord and strife for all, or worse slavery for the blacks than they have ever yet known, in either of which events our prosperity is severed at its roots.

This line, in few words, is the division of the whites and the blacks of the South into two hostile camps, working in opposite directions and seeking opposite ends — the whites damning the blacks and their allies, and the blacks presenting a solid front of opposition against the whites. That this state of affairs is not healthy or natural is apparent to all, but the fact that it undeniably exists proves that there must be some deep-seated causes in operation to produce such an effect, and it behooves us to inquire diligently and candidly what these causes are; and if of our making, to do our part for their removal, or if of others' making, to seek to produce amendment in them. But truth, and not party, must be our object.

It is a common impression among the whites that this color line is drawn solely by the blacks, and *ap-*

parently this is so, but before deciding, it will be well to examine the facts and judge accordingly.

Naturally, there are many antagonisms in the problem. Thus:

Former masters,	Former slaves,
White,	Black,
Beauty,	Ugliness,
Wealth,	Indigence,
Knowledge,	Ignorance,
Intelligence,	Stupidity,
Refinement,	Degradation,

and many others unnecessary to mention, and these of themselves are sufficient to create broad and deep lines of demarkation, which would require years of patient wisdom for their eradication.

These are natural and mutual antagonisms for which we are not responsible, but there are other antagonisms which are strictly artificial, and are of our own making, and for which somebody is responsible.

Thus we (the Southern whites) opposed with all our might

Negro emancipation,
Negro civil rights,
Negro ballot,
Negro office-holding,
Negro jurymen,

— and the Negroes obtained all these cardinal and essential rights in spite of our most determined and bitter opposition.

In Virginia, we enacted degrading legislation, aimed solely at the Negroes, namely, the

Whipping-post,
Chain-gang,

the repeal of which was against our wishes. We also required a poll-tax prerequisite to voting, and we repealed that law solely because it was found to keep more whites than blacks from the polls.

And we still maintain in North Carolina a county government law expressly designed and administered so that Negroes are totally deprived of the benefit of their county majorities. And we still maintain in South Carolina a system of electoral machinery designed especially to deprive the Negroes of their political voice, and so worked that the end is effectually accomplished.

We also proclaim, both by words and acts, that Negroes shall not hold office of any kind, however small — our leading paper of Virginia, the Richmond *Dispatch*, expressing the idea by saying that as long as a white man capable of holding an office can be found, no Negro, however worthy and capable, shall be appointed — that is to say, of the six or more millions of Negroes, of six millions of citizens, that not one of them, whatever his merits, shall hold the smallest office in the land of his nativity, in the home of his birth. Unclean, unclean is the sentence, and unclean shall they ever be, if we can prevail; our sole terms to the Negro being perpetual inferiority and degradation, and an acquiescence by the Negroes in this degraded status.

But we will not call this drawing the color line, for the Negroes are the ones who do this.

But, then, let us see how the Negroes acted in the

days of their supremacy, and how they act now. Even in reconstruction times, when everything favored Negro supremacy, the Negroes by no means confined offices and official favors to their own color, but generally entrusted them to the whites. And at present, how do they act where they have control? Speaking for Virginia, no one questions that the Negroes enjoy a free vote and a fair count, and that they are the strength of the Republican party. Now, for four years, beginning with 1878, the Republican party had absolute control of the state,[1] but during that period was not every office, from senator to county judges, and even to clerks in the state capitol, given to the whites; and did not they elect white congressmen where their majority was unquestioned, and did they not also, as a rule, send white men to the Legislature from counties they controlled? And now that Republican supremacy has disappeared in the state, how do the Negroes act in the so-called black counties? Do they say to the whites, as the whites say to them, "No whites need apply"? No; on the contrary, they give the whites about every sheriff, every treasurer, every commissioner of the revenue, every county and every circuit court clerk, and they content themselves with being justices of the peace, janitors, and such like. Whatever their other defects, the Negroes, as a rule, have sense enough to select for office-holders the best whites they can find in their own party, and in default of them, they select the best Democrats attainable.

But, we say, they cannot fill the offices because of

---

[1] The Readjuster party of Virginia formed a coalition with the Republicans in this period. (Ed.)

incompetency, or, if capable, from inability to give requisite security. This is true in great measure, but still they could, as so many white politicians seek continually to do, wreck if they could not rule, and they might say, as we do with regard to their holding office, rather than that the whites shall hold the offices, we will let things go to the devil; but no, they do not draw the color line, but freely bestow the offices upon the whites. From this example of the action of the Negroes in Virginia, we should dismiss as unmanly and unwarrantable fears that ruin and disaster follow in the train of the free, untrammeled suffrage of the blacks. If a free ballot and a fair count mean Negro rule, then we have Negro rule in all of Tidewater Virginia. Now, who draws the color line, whites or blacks? Each man shall answer for himself.

We frequently hear the expression, "Oh, that the color line could be broken, and that the Negroes would divide their votes between the Democratic and Republican parties"; and when we say so, we fondly imagine that the Negroes are the only sinners, and we never for a moment suspect that we may be the sole impediment to this much desired division. It is greatly to be wished that this color line could be broken, for as long as it remains intact it is a great injury to our welfare and a great menace to our peace and prosperity; and as long as it lasts, statesmanship is absolutely impossible, and we will be perpetually consulting expediency, availability, and everything else but right and reason.

Now, as long as we maintain our present attitude, let us see what is the prospect of dividing the Negro vote; or why should they vote for the Democrats, and why should they not vote for the Republicans. In the first place, who gave them freedom, the ballot, civil rights, etc.? The Republicans. Who opposed all these things? We, the whites, who stand for the Democrats. Who raised them from slaves, with their lives belonging to others, to full-fledged citizens of the greatest country on earth? The Republicans. And who opposed this elevation? We, the whites.

And secondly, who extends them a helping hand politically, who offers them encouragement politically, and who promises to perfect and render practicable all the rights and privileges they now theoretically enjoy? The Republicans. And who says to them, "You Negroes are not only now a degraded and inferior race, but you are also incapable of material elevation; therefore, you must be content to occupy permanently and eternally an inferior and degraded condition — you must be satisfied to be our menial servants, to be our hewers of wood and our drawers of water — this is the best we will do for you"? We, the whites.

Now, with these facts before us, how can we expect the Negroes to be anything but enemies to the Democrats and friends to the Republicans? We cannot; and change is impossible as long as waters seek the sea or the skies water the earth. And, pray, who is to blame for this ominous and dangerous state of affairs? We or the Negroes?

Again: As we are kind to the Negroes individually, and as we do them many a service, when we ask or expect them to vote with us we are greatly surprised and accuse them of ingratitude if, as they generally do, they decline. But we forget that most of our kindness to the Negroes proceeds from the standpoint of condescension and of assumed caste superiority, and we expect it to be received with humility and from a feeling of acknowledged caste inferiority; and if not so received by the Negroes, they are thought impudent and impertinent, and the fountain of our kindness soon dries up. So when we ask the Negro to vote with us he says to himself, "Yes, Mr. A. is a mighty good man, and he has done me a heap of kindness, but Mr. A. belongs to white man's party, and he's always gwine with his party, which is always dead against nigger. No, can't vote with him; must stick to my friends." It is as natural for the Negro to vote against us as it is for us to vote against carpet-baggers and South-haters.

Again: We think it very heinous for Negroes to persecute Negroes for voting with us. Why should we? See what we do when Southern Democrats turn Republicans. We do not, at least in Virginia, persecute them physically, but at the very rumor of one doing so, we look askance at him and turn the cold shoulder to him; and when the rumor becomes confirmed, sociability ceases, friendship cools, and he unmistakably loses social caste.

Now, these changes take place towards people whose party does not threaten us with perpetual inferiority and degradation. We cannot brook any turning to the Republicans, and yet we think it monstrous when Negroes ostracize their own color, and even visit them with pains and penalties, for joining those whose watchword for the six millions of Negroes is eternal degradation and perpetual inferiority. Strange, passing strange!

To break this dark and ominous color line rests with us, but we can obliterate it only by treating the Negroes with equality and impartiality, and by according them cheerfully all the rights that we ourselves enjoy; and, unless we do so, the day is not far remote when we shall find that the scepter has departed from our hands never to return until a new and wiser generation shall have come upon the stage.

Oligarchy, caste, vassalage, are the regnant spirit in the greater portion of the South, and no country can prosper under their weight. To prosper, their galling chains must be sundered; and if ever they are broken, as they surely will be, mixed schools, by disseminating correct ideas of personal liberty and equality, will bear an honorable part. Until the Negro sees and feels that he can of right enter the school attended by his white neighbor, the brand of degradation must eat into and consume his soul.

CHAPTER XXI

The Dangers Threatened by the Present Condition of the Negro — Dangers from Within — Enmity and Bitterness of Blacks to Whites; Causes Thereof — Whites Opposed every Right Gained by Negroes — Special Legislation against Blacks — Whites Deliberately Increasing these Feelings — How? — By Seeking to Educate the Blacks to be Content with an Inferior Status — Should be Educated to the Utmost or every Negro School should be Closed — Three Alternatives — Give the Blacks an Inch and they will take an Ell — No — Why Reconstruction Days Impossible — What has Occurred in Virginia.

Although the South presents a quiet and peaceful aspect, we have no assurance that this condition of the undisputed supremacy of the whites, and the undisputed inferiority and degradation of the blacks, will continue indefinitely, because this very state of affairs which seems so satisfactory to our short-sighted selfishness has produced, and is daily producing, in the hearts of six millions of fellow-citizens a vast mass of smoldering enmity and bitterness, only awaiting a favorable opportunity to display itself. We have raised up an enemy, silent and sullen, at our very doors, who, though he will never conquer, stands ever ready to vex and harass, and to league with those who, for any cause, seek to upturn the present order of affairs.

Inferior as the Negroes undeniably are, they have sense enough to see that the whites, as a caste, are their constant and inveterate foes, not that individually they are harsh and cruel, but they know that this kindness springs mainly from the same benevolence that prompts consideration for their horses and cattle, for their cats and dogs. They know that the whites will not maltreat them, provided they throw up their hands and quietly submit to arbitrary will, but they also know that if they do not, they go to the wall, irrespective of right or wrong. They remember that the whites fought a long and bloody war, not desisting until absolutely exhausted, or until they literally had reached the last ditch, to keep them in servitude; that they organized a Ku-Klux to render their freedom nugatory; that they violently opposed the Federal amendment granting suffrage; that civil rights were conferred in spite of all their efforts, and that generally they have opposed everything tending to their elevation. They know, also, that when this opposition is quiescent, it is only dormant, not dead, and that it springs into full vigor at the slightest alarm, for did not the appointment by Governor Cameron,[1] of Virginia, of a few Negro school trustees suffice to hurl from power at the first subsequent election the

[1] William E. Cameron (1842-1927), elected governor by the Readjuster party in 1881, held the office in 1882-1884. (Ed.)

Republican party, which then controlled every branch of the state government?

They know also that this opposition of the whites is still in full vigor, depriving them of some of their most valuable rights; for is there not now in full operation in North Carolina what is known as the County Government Law, whereby, for the purpose of depriving the Negroes of the management of local affairs in counties where they are in the majority, the people of *all* the counties are debarred the right of electing their most important county officers? And do they not also know that the whites of the Palmetto State, for the same purpose of depriving the Negroes of their electoral franchise, have instituted complicated elective machinery, whereby a number of ballot boxes, seven,[2] it is thought, must be opened at each and every precinct, and if a ballot is put in the wrong box it is lost, thus hindering and bewildering and practically disfranchising thousands of voters? Imagine seven ballot boxes being necessary to secure a fair election in South Carolina, when only one is needful in Virginia, and everywhere else. They know, too, that the whites jealously exclude them from all offices, however small, unless it be to clean spittoons and to do other such menial and degrading work. Now, these and many other things, among them the whipping-post, chain-gang, and prepayment of poll-tax before voting, all now happily repealed, convince the Negroes that the whites, as a caste, are hostile to everything tending to their free, equal and independent citizenship; and since they so believe, can we be sur-

[2] Actually the South Carolina law required eight ballot boxes. (ED.)

prised at their persistent and even blind opposition to
everything advocated by the ruling caste, or that ran-
cor and bitterness necessarily smolder in their bosoms?
If they listened to the whites, it would be a most
wonderful instance of unnaturalism. Hence the whites,
instead of having six millions of friends and co-workers in prosperity, as they should have if they showed
only a willingness to elevate the Negro, have that
number of secret foes in their midst.

But here we are confronted by a singular fact. Instead of seeking to diminish and finally eradicate
this enmity, we are taking deliberate measures to increase it. Indeed! How? Simply by seeking to educate
the Negroes, but not to educate them to the full measure of manhood and citizenship, but to educate them
to be still inferiors, to be still subordinate to ourselves, and to be content to occupy the lower stratum
while we occupy the upper. Education is not only to
fill the mind with knowledge, but to make men and
citizens in the highest sense of the word; but our idea
of the education of the Negro is to load him with
knowledge, but to abridge the process of making him
the best attainable man and citizen, and to arrest his
mental growth at a point permanently inferior to
our own, and, after having done this, to expect the
Negro to be satisfied. Although this is an impossibility,
because a flat contradiction, we do not see it, but we
go on and furnish not only common and high schools,
but also normal schools and colleges. We should stop
at once all education of the Negro, shut up his every
public school, and forbid all private Negro schools,
unless we are prepared to carry his education to its
highest attainable point, and are willing to accept all

its consequences — for every increase of education only increases and intensifies his present discontent and enmity. How? Because the more uneducated we keep him the less he perceives his wretched and degraded lot; therefore, the less dissatisfied with it, and the less enmity to his superiors. But educate or elevate him ten per cent, what then? That elevation, slight as it is, enables him to see more clearly his degraded condition, and to feel more keenly his disadvantages, and to be still more indisposed to his superiors. We go twenty per cent — sight, feeling, enmity, are all intensified. At fifty per cent, being willing that the Negroes be that much superior, but that much inferior, we call a halt.

But at this point we find ourselves in a double dilemma. The Negroes are now in a position to see tenfold their degraded lot, and to feel tenfold their disadvantages, and when the command "Halt!" is heard they will be little disposed to respond "Yea!" and being now more enlightened, they will be stronger, and they will demand a further advance to sixty, seventy, and will not be content until the full hundred mark is reached. But the whites will then be at a disadvantage, for having gone fifty per cent, they can give no *reason* for not conceding the demand for seventy, and then for eighty, and then for the full hundred. We should stop at once and retrace our steps or go forward to the end, for three alternatives await our present course. The Negroes, being partially elevated, looking behind and seeing the horrible pit whence they have escaped, and looking forward and seeing the immense benefits to be gained and almost within their reach, will never cease their efforts until they have gained the whole one hundred per cent, and are as free and as equal citizens as the proudest whites. This is one alternative. Or the whites, opposing all further advance, will strenuously resist, and becoming embittered by opposition will not rest until they have succeeded in completely disarming the blacks and reducing them to a condition of absolute and complete subordination and degradation. This is another alternative. Or neither side being strong enough to have its way, there must be continual and alternate defeats and victories, advances and retreats — a perpetual strife and discord — and factions must rend the community, in which event the state must languish and prosperity disappear, for prosperity dwells only where concord reigns. This is the third alternative. The first means peace, happiness, prosperity for all; the other two mean strife, sorrow, adversity for all. This, however, is the age of reason, and we may therefore look forward with confidence to the day when the first alternative, after many difficulties, delays, and dangers, shall wear the crown of victory. We older ones will not see that day, but our grandchildren will, for the light of coming day already irradiates the eastern sky.

But what of this smoldering enmity? It may mean that society may at times be upset, and it may mean disturbances of greater or less violence, and it may mean only sullen but silent discontent; but it does mean that the Negroes will always be on the alert to welcome divisions in the white ranks, and to coalesce with any faction, whether they be worthy citizens rebelling against corrupt ring rule and seeking the public welfare, or merely unscrupulous adventurers in search of their own selfish ends, for Negroes will naturally say, Change for us has no terrors, for we cannot possibly be worsted, being at the bottom already; on the contrary, change for us is welcome because it may bring advantage. The whites, therefore, instead of bending all their time, thoughts and energies towards promoting prosperity, will be engaged in watching the Negroes to prevent such coalitions, or, having been formed, in circumventing them. Instead of working, the whites will rather be constantly on guard, and living, as it were, in entrenched camps. But granting the whites long and undisputed lease of power, the danger is not removed; only delayed, but intensified. Long lease of power begets bosses; bosses beget abuses; abuses beget frauds of all kinds in order to perpetuate themselves, and frauds, becoming unbearable, finally beget factions, upheavals, or even revolutions; and when faction or revolution controls public affairs, there is no predicting to what length resentment and revenge may not go.

But most people will say, "Give the Negroes an inch, and they will take an ell; unless we deprive them of their political rights, their numerical superiority in some states and coalition in other states with ambitious and unscrupulous whites will give them complete control of the South, and we will soon see again reconstruction days, when, led by scalawags and carpet-baggers, they wrecked all they controlled." Such reasoning is, however, altogether illogical and chimerical, and is begotten of unmanly timidity. It requires like conditions to produce like effects, but neither the times, nor the Negroes, nor even the whites, are anything like, and can never be like, what they were for a few years after the war. Then, with the Negroes just enfranchised and enthused with most extravagant expectations, nothing was improbable or even impossible; but when the conduct of the Negroes and their allies is compared with that of the peasantry of France during the Revolution, as set forth by Taine, one is amazed at the little evil they wrought. During that awful period France was plundered and brought to the verge of starvation by her own children; her best people were exiled, murdered or guillotined, and her fair bosom was converted into a frightful scene of arson, pillage and bloodshed; but the Negroes and their allies merely stole. Reconstruction days are as much of the past as are the fearful times of Tiberius, of the Inquisition, of Thomas Cromwell, of the Reign of Terror, and are no more likely to return; and those who seek to excite our fears by preaching their return are either blind, timid, or corrupt, and are unworthy of our confidence. The Negroes have learned a great deal the past twenty-five years; they have learned in some degree that their own welfare is bound up in good government, and they would therefore be willing to hearken to and co-operate with us, and thus keep affairs in the hands of the worthiest, did we but show slight regard to all their rights and privileges; and the only sure way for us permanently to maintain control is to make them sharers with us in the honors and the privileges of government. Our present attitude will forever repel them and make them deaf to our most persuasive solicitations; change that attitude to one of justice and fair dealing, and enough will come to us to banish forever the dread of so-called Negro rule.

Having seen what may occur, let us now recall what has occurred. Several years ago there was a split in the Democratic party of Virginia on the subject of the state debt. The minority, though led by able men, chief of whom was General William Mahone, found itself helpless; but as the leaders were ambitious as well as able, they seceded and sought the assistance of the Negroes, who responded promptly to the invitation, not that they knew or cared anything about the debt, but they knew the Democratic party was their enemy, and they knew that they could not be injured and might be benefited; or that if they could not in the end shout victory, they could at least sing revenge. In a short time the minority, with the aid of the Negroes, gained complete mastery of the state. A clean sweep of every office was made. Judges, school superintendents, and even directors of eleemosynary institutions, were turned out or legislated out, and in a year or two the Democratic party, which had controlled the state from its birth, was as impotent as it is in the Green Mountain State. Virginia was now a satrapy, and Mahone was its satrap. He set up one and he pulled down another, like a Pharaoh; he absolutely controlled all Federal appointments within the state, and he might, with great truth, say, as did the Grand Monarque, "I am the State." Bitter factions rent the state, families were divided, father from son, and brother from brother, and a great gloom settled upon the whites. They felt as if they had passed beneath portals which were inscribed, "He who enters here, let him bid adieu to hope," for hope had seemed to have deserted the land. But even these were not reconstruction days. Such times, however, are liable to occur at any time as long as we say to the Negroes, as we do to our pointer dogs, "Down, down," followed with the lash if obedience is not instant. To escape such dangers, there is only one way — respect all the Negroes' rights as scrupulously as we do our own.

CHAPTER XXII

The Dangers Threatened by the Present Condition of the Negro — Dangers from Without — Dangers of Sectionalism Not Removed by Emancipation, but Direction Changed — Weakness of the South Sure to Continue and to Increase — Tables Showing This — Constitution Impotent to Protect — Partisan Majority in Congress can Absolutely Disfranchise Every Southern State.

Although sectional divisions on the line of slavery are gone, sectional divisions on the line of geography and interest are still in full vigor. There are yet New England, Middle State, Western, Northwestern, and Pacific sections, all more or less united in interest and blood, and there is yet the Southern section, which is diverse in interest and lineage from the other sections.

In matters of national legislation, therefore, there are likely to be two great sections, namely, the South on one hand, and the North and West on the other hand; and what one section *especially* favors, the other section will probably oppose; and as sectional legislation has always been a great, and, we may say, an inevitable evil, so we must expect it in the future, for whatever is or seems to be for the advantage of a section will be advocated by that section, though the whole army of wise men and saints should arise from the dead and pronounce it wrong. Change conditions, but not change location, and New England and Pennsylvania would be for free trade, and the South would be for protection. The lever to move the world that Archimedes sought, but never found, is interest, or seeming interest. Take away our seeming interest in heaven, and every church will be closed in twelve months; and the pastors will be roughing it in the world instead of basking in the smiles and feeding on the adulations of the "sisters."

Having, then, still to deal with sections and sectional interests, let us inquire what are the prospects of the South for increasing, or even holding, her own in this sectional race or strife. Adding Delaware, Maryland, West Virginia, Kentucky and Missouri to the eleven Southern states, the population in 1880 was 17,622,381 as against 31,748,959 in the remaining twenty- two states, and the area is respectively 901,740 and 1,185,020 square miles. Present representation in congress is — Senate, 32 and 44, and House, 121 and 204.

Now, granting an equal ratio of increase of population in the two great sections, the proportion of the representatives in 1890 will, on the basis of thirty per cent increase in population, be 157 and 265, and in 1900, on the same basis, 203 and 344, or the majority against us now of 83 will be increased to 108 and 141.

But this is not all. Back of the states lie a number of territories, and before long they will be taking their places in the halls of legislation. Let us see how they will naturally divide as for or against the South:

FOR THE SOUTH		AGAINST THE SOUTH	
New Mexico	122,580	Utah	84,970
Arizona	113,000	Washington	69,180
Indian Territory	64,690	Dakota	149,100
		Idaho	84,800
		Montana	146,080
		Wyoming	97,890
Total	300,270	Total	632,020

In course of time, therefore, certainly within ten years, the South as a section will be still further weakened — that is, relatively, as one to two, for at the most she can expect to gain only six senators and 300,270 square miles, while the opposing section gains twelve senators and 632,020 square miles. If Dakota succeeds in being divided the gain will be six to fourteen. In the House our relative increase will not be any greater and most probably much less. As showing that the new states will likely be anti-Southern, we note that nine states have been added to the Union since the annexation of Texas, and all except West Virginia are bitter Republican states. These are the opposing forces the South will have to meet on questions of a sectional character; and what is she going to do if they should arise, as they are sure to do?

The South feels safe under the shelter of the constitution, and allowing that that sacred instrument will not again be wrested from its true intent and meaning, although our past experience should teach us to place little dependence upon constitutions, is she then safe from partial, hostile or even revolutionary measures? Granting she has not only a majority but the whole of the Supreme Court, and granting she has the President too, she is not safe if sectionalism becomes aroused, and her safety line is not reached until she controls Supreme Court, Senate and House. How is this? Because both the Senate and the House are absolute judges of the election and qualification of their own members. Let us see, and let us take for example the denial of suffrage to the blacks. The South makes no denial of the charge, but defends it on the plea of necessity. This plea may satisfy us, and it will, because it *appears* to be for our benefit; but suppose the other sections are not satisfied, and that they demand a free vote and a fair count in the South, as well as everywhere else; and suppose, further, that the Republican party gains the House, as it already controls the Senate, what may it do? We will take for example the State of Georgia, and suppose that after the House is organized contestants from some or all the districts *allege* intimidation, what may follow?

Looking at the returns and finding that fewer than 30,000 voters elected in 1886 ten congressmen, or, indeed, without looking at them at all, the House may unseat every congressman, and who — Supreme Court, Senate, President — can prevent? And what can prevent it from doing the same to every Southern state, and completely deprive them of representation, or let them be represented by Republican contestants? Nothing except the public sentiment of its members' own sections. And all the Senate has to do is to refuse every Southern senator, on the ground that the legislature of his state was not elected by a fair vote. The South will then be in a bad dilemma, either unrepresented or misrepresented, and there will be no limit to the arbitrary or revengeful legislation that may be enacted, and never again will a Democratic President be elected by her vote. To be weak and right is miserable; to be weak and wrong is deplorable. In the first case, one's right will be a powerful defense against wrong; in the second case, one has no defense, and his misfortune will excite no sympathy, but on the contrary, the verdict will be, served him right.

If the South wishes to bring this evil upon herself, let her continue in her present course, and she will have her wish gratified by the year 1900. The whites may by that time see themselves disfranchised by rejection of their representatives, or they may see themselves misrepresented by contestants who are most likely to be incompetent and revengeful. But if the whites wish to retain control of affairs they cannot begin too soon, not only to permit, but to encourage, the blacks to use their franchise freely and fully. Some congressmen and legislators will undoubtedly be lost thereby, but better many of them be lost, and thus mitigate the just enmity of the Negroes and disarm sectional majorities, only too eager for pretexts. Sectionalism is powerful and irresistible when founded on right, but when founded on error, time and discussion will rob it of its venom.

While we disfranchise we give sectionalism a powerful lever to root us up, but when we give a free vote to every citizen and a fair count we need not fear sectionalism or anything else, for our right will be a panoply to protect us from all assaults. No man, no party, no section, can afford to plant itself upon a fallacy, much less upon a wrong; and when the South takes her stand upon practical denial of suffrage to her Negro citizens she commits a monumental wrong, which must be atoned for by many tribulations. The people, the world, we ourselves, though nursing and defending our own wrongs, are opponents and enemies of the wrongs of others, and on this principle we shall have not only the violent opposition of the other sections, but they will be upheld by the sympathies of the world. As a general observes with delight the blunders of his adversary, and gloats over his victory in advance, so we may imagine our political enemies rejoicing over our wrong movements, and gloating over the idea that, in a few years, by the natural increase of their section, they will again by our errors be placed not only again in control of the National Government, but also in absolute control of the South itself. We may then call upon the Supreme Court, but our enemies will laugh at us, and, like the prophets and the priests of Baal, they will tell us, call louder, you don't call loud enough; the Court is asleep or on a vacation; for by the power of Congress to decide upon the qualifications of its members, they can keep out every one of our representatives, or admit only those whose sentiments suit them. They will not even be under the necessity of tampering with the Supreme Court, as was done during Grant's administration, because it will be impotent and despised. When the other sections simply demand that the South shall allow the same unrestricted vote and the same untampered count in the election of congressmen and of legislators that elect senators, we cannot say in reply, Oh! the bloody shirt, but we shall be speechless.

The South would make a tremendous ado, and very rightly, too, if a Northern oligarchy of half the population were to claim and assume the right to vote for the whole population in the election of national representatives, and it would make still greater ado if an oligarchy of manufacturers were to exercise this right; but there is no substantial difference between this and what the South does in relation to Negro suffrage. The other sections will see, if they do not already, that they are right, and they will not cease their efforts until the South yields voluntarily or is forced, and then after the South yields through compulsion, we cannot blame others if we are forced to take back seats until we have gone through a long probation. Better surrender now with the honors of the war, or rather with the honors of right, than to wait for years and then surrender at discretion. If there is any truth in experience these are the only two alternatives.

If the South intends to maintain her present posture of caste and practical denial of Negro suffrage, she must, in addition to stopping at once all education of the Negroes, place a close and lofty cordon around herself, not only to prevent all ingress, but also all egress — that is to say, we must shut ourselves out from the world as completely as China did for many centuries, and we must now, in these days of light and civilization, imitate China in the days of ignorance and barbarism. She must at once cease her pleadings, humiliating in their despairing urgency, to

Northern people to come down and take possession of and develop her resources, although manhood and a very moderate sense of pride should make her develop them herself; but she should repel all who voluntarily come, and she should also forbid her citizens passing her boundaries and seeing what the world is thinking, saying and doing. As oxygen in the economy of nature, so is light, thought, intelligence to Southern politico-social economy. As oxygen corrodes and finally devours the dying and the dead, as it is destruction to everything that does not keep step with progress towards perfection, and will thus, in time, perhaps, by its removal of wrecks, obstructions and decaying matters, produce perfection, so light, thought, intelligence will as inevitably upset or overturn everything that cannot approve itself on the ground of right and reason. If, therefore, we let others come in, our system of caste and denial of suffrage is at once put to the test of right and reason; and if we let our citizens go out into the world, their ideas on the same subject are at once put on the defense by everything they see in the moving, stirring and progressive outside world; and if our defenses are weak, then, like flimsy barriers against a current, they must inevitably give way: those who come among us, being born with different ideas, and those of our sons who have gone abroad and imbibed the spirit of the world, both co-operating to tear down what we are now so fondly and blindly upholding.

What reason can we give for our present stand but the fear that something may occur that would be injurious to the present order of affairs? This is no better reason, but is the very same that has been offered since man assembled into a rude community, by all abuses, by all tyrants, by all despots. All these oppose change solely on the ground that the pleasant order of affairs of which they are the principal beneficiaries may be altered to their disadvantage, and to maintain the *status quo* they resort to stripes, imprisonments, dungeons, and scaffolds. As light, intelligence, reason spread, they, like oxygen in the physical world, corrode and finally consume all such fallacies and sophisms, and at last evolve from corruptions, abuses and tyrannies of all kinds the beautiful and beneficent structure of liberty and equality, when all can say they are equal citizens of an equal government. But the South cannot stand this acid test of light, intelligence and reason, and, therefore, if she intends to maintain her present status, she must, in addition to all her other methods, exclude all from without and constrain all within to remain within.

CHAPTER XXIII

*What of the Future? — Present Status Likely
to Pass Away — Day Breaks.*

If there be truth in the aphorism that "Where truth
and error are free to combat, truth is sure finally to
prevail," then there can be no doubt as to the ultimate
issue of the conflict between caste and equality: caste
is the essence of the political and social Southern problem, denial of the ballot being merely an incident of
caste. On this question we are not left alone to reasoning, but we have as well experience in the world at
large; but better still, we have experience in the South
itself.

As already said, the world, meaning thereby individuals, communities and nations — the world, which
is no meaningless term, but, in these modern days of
quick communication, is a vast engine for the expression and dissemination of social and political influence,
although it may be obstinately wedded to its own particular evils and abuses — is strongly inclined to force
virtue on others and compel them to correct their
abuses. All the world's a stage, doubtless, but all the
world is likewise, in respect of abuses, a number of
beleaguered camps, into which others are perpetually
pouring hot shot and exploding bombs, shattering de-

fenses and uprooting errors and abuses of every kind; and so, if the South determines to maintain her present *status,* so foreign to modern enlightenment, she must prepare to defend her ground against all comers, for she may be sure that when the world is attacking other people's errors and abuses, she, too, will find adversaries at every point of the compass. People feel that when they are attacking others' errors, faults, vices, they are somehow condoning their own shortcomings, and, as the world will have the same feeling when attacking the errors and abuses of the South, we may be sure that the world will come up to the assault with great alacrity. The South, then, should be very sure of its ground before inviting the onslaught, for mere heavy battalions have a tendency to attract the favor of Providence; but heavy battalions supported by right, reason and intelligence are absolutely sure to conquer. If these truths are "self-evident, that all men are created equal; that they are endowed by their Creator with certain unalienable rights; that among these are life, liberty and the pursuit of happiness," then we have no defense for that caste upon which Southern society is built, or for denying to many, or even to a few, rights which we claim for the whites alone. But, denying these truths to be self-evident, or even denying them to be truths at all, what defense can we offer?

Shall we say color? We shall then be forced to define what we mean by color — whether we mean only the pure Caucasian, or the Caucasian and Semitic, or the Caucasian, Semitic and Mongolian, or the Caucasian, Semitic, Mongolian and Red Indian. We will be compelled not only to draw the line somewhere, but we shall be compelled to give sound reasons for drawing the line at the division we select. And will it be possible to do this? And if a *majority* today decides against black, and tomorrow against yellow, why may not a majority decide on another day to discriminate against one branch of the Caucasian, and again, as did the Know-Nothings, against all Caucasians who lived beyond certain limits of a small portion of North America? We can't defend color for a moment unless we contend for segregating every small portion of the human family, and decide in favor of reverting the civilized world to its original savage and barbaric elements, for "color," if carried out, leads logically and inevitably to this.

But we may take this stand: The Negroes are ignorant, are lazy, are mendacious, are dishonest, are licentious, and are therefore utterly unworthy of social and political equality. Granted, and granted to the fullest extent; but the more degraded, the world will say, the greater obligation resting upon us to rescue them from their blighted and brutalized condition. We cannot deport them, because they are too many, and we cannot get rid of them in any other way. They are with us to remain, and they are citizens, and the world will make it its business to see that they are not arbitrarily kept in their present condition. We can no more defend our attitude towards the Negroes than could the Algerian corsairs defend their attitude to the Christian world; than can despots defend their attitude to their subjects, or than can state churches and powerful nobility defend their attitude to the people — all of which have passed or will pass away, and so will pass away the attitude of the whites to the blacks.

Caste will struggle hard, as it always does when its privileges are endangered, to maintain the present *status;* but all its efforts will be in vain, and it must fall before the assaults of the world, founded, as these assaults are, upon right, reason and material good. The battle will be long and obstinate; but darkness, oppression and injustice will, and must, go down before the assaults directed against them from all points of the enlightened world. Victory may and will be deferred and delayed, but it is sure.

But, as already said, we have not to depend upon reasoning; we have experience for our guide. Virginia is much ahead of her Southern sisters in acknowledging the rights of the Negroes; but this is not because Virginians are superior naturally to their brethren, but simply because Virginia is nearer to the world, and is therefore more affected by its enlightening influences than are the more remote states; and the more she comes in contact with the world, the more fully will all the rights of the Negro be accorded, and the greater will be their elevation, and the greater will be her prosperity. And what comes to pass in Virginia will also, under enlightening influences, come to pass later in the other states, till finally distinctions of race and caste will disappear; society will become tolerably homogeneous and will not be torn by conflicting and contending interests, and only such social distinctions will survive as we see at present in private life, where we associate only with those whom inclination selects. When society becomes homogeneous, then and only then shall we behold the full and complete prosperity of the South.

CHAPTER XXIV

To the North — In Vain to Preach Right until Interest is Shown to be on the Side of Right — Example of England and India, and of the Manufacturing States and Rest of the Country.

While the elevation of the Negro is primarily a Southern question, it is not wholly so. You, too, if not so vitally, are also vitally interested therein; and I now address you on the same momentous subject.

You will observe that I have appealed little, if at all, to right, justice, morals, or religion, but that the burden of the argument has been dollars and cents, and the exhortation to elevate has not been because this was great or noble, but simply because it would be profitable. And this keynote of appeal to the pocket, which many will consider as ignoble, was deliberately struck, not because Southerners are worse than others or less susceptible to arguments of the loftiest kind, but simply because all experience proves that human nature must be interested on its material side before its intellectual and moral instincts can be permanently stimulated. In order to move men to practice justice and right they must first be convinced that it will be profitable for them to do so. Occasionally the individual by a supreme effort will sacrifice a great deal in order to do right, but never does a community voluntarily do right at the expense of seeming interest.

For example: grand as Great Britain is, leader of civilization as she has been, foe to slavery everywhere as she was and is, cynosure of all peoples who struggle for liberty or aspire to constitutional government, will she, the lighthouse of the world, loose her iron grasp from the millions of India whom she euphemistically calls by the same name as Englishmen themselves — namely, subjects — as long as she finds it profitable to rule them by the sword, sheathed it may be, but ever ready to leap from its scabbard and to slay right and left? Never! In such case the cry of right is as the infant's wail in the hurricane's blast. Although Great Britain has no more right to hold these millions in subjection than these millions have to hold Great Britain — and every intelligent Englishman will say, True — yet does not this same Englishman, does not the Imperial Government, does not even Gladstone himself, as fair and honest a statesman as ever lived, uphold and defend this slavery of innumerable millions? And why? Simply because it is to the material good of England to hold them in chains.

Great Britain and India are linked together not by ties of friendship, equality, and mutual interest, but rather by bands like the bridge built by Satan for the ruin of man from the gates of hell to the new-created earth. They are, as it were, bound together by a vast siphon, one end of which gathers up the riches of India and the other end discharges them in a broad, lavish and perennial stream into the pockets of Englishmen. In the face of such gain, whistle to the winter's storm, rebuke ocean's billows mountains high dashing against the shore, call upon the dead slumbering in costly tombs or in graves unmarked by mound or slightest shrub, and you will be heeded sooner than by England when you speak of the rights of India, the sweat and blood of whose helpless children are coined into golden ducats for the benefit of her masters. In view of this benefit it seems to Englishmen no inconsistency to despoil the natives of almost everything except a girdle around the loins and a turban upon the head, and then spend a small portion of this enforced tribute in sending missionaries to convert them to the religion of their conquerors. No! They think they are thereby serving God acceptably. Mammon blinds the eye to every consideration of justice and equity, and we can get a hearing for these noble virtues only when we can show that our own welfare will be enhanced by observing them.

And so it is vain to preach to New England and Pennsylvania the wrong — iniquity is not too strong a word — of wresting the legislative machinery of a common country to selfish ends as long as they find their riches increased enormously thereby. By this arbitrary and unjust legislative process they construct huge siphons, not one, as in the case of India and England, but many, all of which have their discharging ends resting upon their states, or rather upon their own particular employments, and their other ends, like monstrous measuring worms, stretch out menacingly and ominously towards the agricultural interests, and, settling upon them everywhere, drain them of their wealth. As long as this impoverishment of the one and this enrichment of the other can be maintained, what matters it to these states, and all similar beneficiaries, at what expense to others this profitable result is obtained? They care not if their legalized exactions bear onerously upon the vast majority, and are literally crushing to the six millions of Southern Negroes, whose welfare the North claims to seek. The Negroes' poverty, great and grinding as it is, excites no commiseration in the breasts of these beneficiaries of partial and arbitrary laws, but on the contrary, through means of these laws they inexorably demand tribute upon all the Negroes wear, upon all tools and implements used in gaining their plain and scanty living, upon their medicines, their books, upon their very Bibles — mind, body, and soul being laid under tribute — a small tribute, perhaps, upon the well-to-do and easy to be borne, but a crushing one to those whose means are more than represented by the widow's two mites.

What do these burdens, heavy and grievous to be borne, matter to those who reap the benefit of them? Nothing. On the contrary, no more satisfied than were the Romans with the spoil and plunder of conquered provinces, they demand more and still more. They exact taxes — partial taxes — not only for the support of government, but they demand, if taxes are not needed for government, taxes for the benefit of themselves — the public revenues to be absolutely thrown away rather than lift the burdens of others — and they literally demand that the world itself be shut out rather than allow any interference with their arbitrary privileges. Preach to such people of the injustice of such a course and you are talking to the deaf. No, not to the deaf, for they are conscious of some atmospheric vibrations, but to the dead, who will hear noth-

88 HE PROSPERITY OF THE SOUTH DEPENDENT

ing less awakening than the blast of Gabriel's trump.
Or, if allowing themselves to think for a moment of
the galling poverty they are perpetuating, and if possible intensifying, among the millions of Negroes, they
quiet their consciences, as do the English in the case of
India, by devoting an infinitesimal fragment of what
they have wrung from these wretched creatures to
sending them the gospel, and a few other thousands to
educate them — mere drops in the sea, and as ineffect-
tual.

The manufacturing states will never surrender their
unrighteous hold upon the national legislature as long
as they find it profitable, be the poverty of the agricultural states never so great; but the agricultural states
themselves will support them until it can be proved to
their satisfaction that so-called protection, in reality,
decreasing their income and increasing their expenses,
is greatly to their injury, and finally leads to their
bankruptcy. Until their material interests are shown to
be injured, wrong, injustice, robbery, iniquity, as applied to so-called protection, will be idle words. Therefore, in my argument, ignoring every other motive, I
have sought only to show that the welfare of the
whites themselves is dependent upon the elevation of
the Negro, and until this is done, to preach to the
whites his elevation is as futile as to preach to Englishmen "Hands off India!" or to New England and
Pennsylvania "Hands off Congress!" Until the ruling sentiment in each region is convinced that equality
is for its good, the Negroes will be practical slaves in
the South, the people of India will be practical slaves
to England, and the people of the United States will be
practical slaves to New England and Pennsylvania.

Unenlightened human nature is the same everywhere — following what seems to be for its interest; but, as self-interest is generally blind, we are more apt to go astray than go right, and therefore it is necessary to study patiently and industriously in order to see where our true interest really lies. Apparent interest is usually forward and obtrusive; real interest is frequently hidden or obscure. The North worships the protection of manufactures; the South worships the protection of men — of a caste. Both are wrong, for each advocates the protection of a part at the expense of the whole.

CHAPTER XXV

The Duty of the North

We must now discuss duties as well as material good — right as well as interest. We have hitherto confined ourselves almost solely to material good, and we have deliberately chosen what some may think a very low standpoint, not because Southerners are not responsive to rights and duties, or not because Northerners are *in esse* better than Southerners, but we have selected this point because all experience proves it vain to preach rights and duties when they are in conflict with what appears to be interest. But we can now discuss the duties of you Northerners toward a large portion of our fellow-citizens, because your material interests are not so intimately involved.

You have duties to perform, and most serious ones, too, in the matter of the elevation of the Negro, and the Negroes have most valid claims upon you, and if you fail to perform them intelligently Nature will demand a strict accounting at your hands. Although your interests are secondary to those of the South, they are yet great, because in a common country one great section cannot languish without the other sections, even the wealthy and prosperous manufacturing sections, suffering also, and if the prosperity of the

South is dependent upon the elevation of the Negro your prosperity is intimately associated with that of the South; hence, if you fail in your part, then you, too, cannot escape the penalty of the South remaining in a stagnant or declining condition in consequence of the Negroes remaining in a state of degradation.

The *argumentum ad hominem*, in common parlance the argument that you do so yourself, although no argument at all, nevertheless performs the work of the most powerful and persuasive argument with the average of mankind. We see this every day. A man declines to be a Christian because some Christians are unfaithful to their profession. The manufacturer reduces his dozens to tens and his pounds to ounces, or adulterates his goods, because other merchants do the same, and the Republican cheats at elections because he believes the Democrat does. If there is any or much self-denial required in doing right most of us decline to do so on the plea that so and so does wrong, and so the greatest impediment in the way of Southerners' being willing to elevate the Negro is your dereliction of duty towards him; because in the North the Negro is frequently treated harshly and unjustly; because he is thrust in the background and is not given a fair chance.

Thus, although the Negro in some parts of the North enjoys many more privileges and exercises many more rights than in the South, especially in the far South, yet he still labors under many arbitrary and artificial disadvantages. Although in the great cities of New York, Boston and Philadelphia, and, most likely, elesewhere, Negro children are admitted as a matter of course to white schools, and although the Negro can travel anywhere without question and can, with exceptions, attend churches, theatres, and official receptions, and put up at hotels, without fear of affront, yet, in the matter of employment or of making a living, he labors under many drawbacks. Thus, while in the South, the Negro may be laborer, mechanic, contractor, or whatnot, and is not molested by his white co-laborers, it is not so with you. In New York City, the Negro is not permitted to make his living except in the most degrading and servile spheres. He cannot work on the streets in public employment, not being allowed even to dig sewer trenches; he cannot work as painter, carpenter, mason, but he may tote bricks up a high ladder for the other men to do all the work; he cannot drive a truck, cab, or car; he cannot, except for his own color, be what his soul most delights in, namely, a barber; and there are many other things he cannot do without danger to his skull. In a word, he can do nothing that Patrick just arrived from the *Ould Counthry* chooses to consider an interference with his pleasures, profits, or even fancies. Evidently, Patrick thinks that if *he* is oppressed at home he ought to be allowed to oppress *somebody*, and finding, upon his arrival in our free and equal country, the weak Negro, he, with the approval, tacit at least, of the North, of the party of great moral ideas, retaliates his wrongs upon him and drives him from all employment but the most menial and the least profitable. The pleasure of being cheated is stated to be as great as the pleasure of cheating, but Patrick evidently believes that the pleasure of oppressing the helpless Negro is infinitely greater than the pleasure of being oppressed in Ireland. The only employments in which the Negroes are allowed freely to engage are not those which develop independence and self-respect, and that bring ease and comfort, but those which breed servility, namely, waiters in hotels, gentlemen's coachmen and valets. Caste pursues and cripples the Negro in the North as it does in the South.

It is probable that the Negro meets with similar treatment generally in the North and West, because an employee of Kirk, a great soap manufacturer in Chicago, told me that on one occasion all Kirk's workmen, about eight hundred, struck because two Negroes were employed in menial positions about the office, and the Negroes had to go. This was chivalrous. Further: A lady who visited Columbus, Ohio, in September, 1888, remarked to me incidentally regarding the wretchedness, and even squalor, of the many Negroes she saw there and in other parts of Ohio, showing that the stronger and more intelligent whites had used the strength of a giant, not to uplift, but to keep the Negroes in a condition of debasement. For Negroes to earn in many parts of the North and West a comfortable and respectable living, they must work in the dark, selfishness seeming to begrudge them anything beyond the fare of the prodigal son — the husks that even the swine refused to eat.

For the North to clear its skirts of the charge of hypocrisy, it must change its own treatment of the Negro; for until it says, Follow my example instead of doing as I exhort, the seed it sows may be good, but it will fall upon hard and stony soil. Negroes being in development but children, the North, if it desires their elevation, must not be indifferent, or even unsympathizing; must not content itself with merely letting things drift, its conscience being satisfied if it places no obstructions in the way; but, as in the case of children, it must set itself resolutely and persistently to encourage them in every way. It is not enough to say, be ye clothed and be ye fed, but actual and practical steps must be taken to put them in the way of earning for themselves that food and that raiment. Instead of narrowing their range of employment, it should be expanded until commensurate with that of the whites. All employments and all offices should be open to them, and especially should all pains, penalties and persecutions inflicted upon them for the sin of color be punished with a firm and unsparing hand. You must create such a public sentiment that the community freely, cordially and practically recognize the fact as *fundamental*, as inalienable, that the Negro enjoy as a right, and not as a privilege or condescension, all the advantages of civil society — such a public sentiment that the most reckless will no more dare to infringe the rights of the Negro than of the white. But you must do more. You must put yourself out of the way to encourage and to stimulate the hope and the self-respect of the Negro, and you must lift from his shoulders the weight of the social structure which still crushes him into the dust. And, if necessary in order to accomplish this great end, all your missionary societies, which are seeking to convert savages and barbarians in all the ends of the earth, should for a few years fix their eyes upon home, and devote all their men, all their means, and all their talents to convert the white heathen at their own doors — to convert themselves, practical heathens or infidels as they are, respecting the rights of the blacks of their own households, and of the many millions in the South. To convert our own household, for whom we are responsible, would seem to be more acceptable service to our Maker than to go to the uttermost parts of the earth in search of those for whom we are slightly, if at all, responsible.

Put your own Negroes in the way of supporting themselves with comfort, throw open all the avenues of life to them, encourage them to enter freely therein, relieve them of the danger and the dread of being robbed, beaten and imposed upon by their ruthless white neighbors; in short, elevate them to the fall stature of citizenship, and then can you appeal with hope of success to your white Southern brethren; but until you do these things, your purest, most unselfish efforts will be looked upon with suspicion, and they will be frustrated by the fatal *argumentum ad hominem*.

Index